Praise for Pasta Pres

"Flavor meets health."

Albuquerque Journal

"A common-sense guide to pasta cookery that packs a powerful amount of variety into 92 pages."

Fresno Bee

"Pasta recipes that not only taste good but are good for you."

Cedar Rapids Gazette

"A clear, no-nonsense, attractive publication."

Los Angeles Times

"Nothing difficult—just good, honest fare for those who like pasta."

Birmingham News

"Simple recipes with easy-to-find ingredients."

Seattle Times

"Designed with both the novice cook and the seasoned pro in mind."

Longview Daily News

"Handsomely organized and illustrated."

Hartford Courant

"Bright look and sensible format makes it a welcome addition for pasta lovers."

Tulsa World

"Innovative recipes, and all under 20% of calories from fat."

Dayton News

"Offers lots of recipes, cooking tips, resources and lore in a lively, user-friendly format."

Asbury Park Press

"All of the recipes can be made by the average cook."

Portland Oregonian

Also by Chris Gluck

Pasta & Garlic: Low-Fat Recipes…That Work!

Pasta Press
(A quarterly magazine for pasta lovers)

Pasta & Vegetables

Low-Fat Recipes...That Work!

Chris Gluck

Illustrations by John Molenaar

Wine Selections by Edmund Osterland, MS

Pasta Press Publishing
San Diego, California

Grateful acknowledgment is made to the following pasta and vegetable lovers, without whom this book would have been impossible.

The recipe on page 24 is reprinted by permission of Patrick Lambert.

The recipes on pages 28, 42, 46 and 78 are reprinted by permission of Arlyn Hackett.

The recipe on page 30 is reprinted by permission of Jeanne Jones.

The recipe on page 48 is reprinted by permission of Grady Spears.

The recipe on page 54 is reprinted by permission of William Anatooskin.

The recipe on page 60 is reprinted by permission of Daniel McKenna.

The recipe on page 62 is reprinted by permission of Frank Garofolo.

The recipes on page 66 and 70 are reprinted by permission of Hugh Carpenter and Ten Speed Press. They were adapted from *Hot Vegetables* (Copyright © 1998) and *Hot Pasta* (Copyright © 1996) by Hugh Carpenter and Teri Sandison.

The recipe on page 76 is reprinted by permission of Adelina Willem.

The recipe on page 82 is reprinted by permission of Stella Fong.

Editing by Linda K. Clarke

Pasta Press Publishing
Post Office Box 3070
San Diego, CA 92163

Publisher's Cataloging-in-Publication

Gluck, Chris.
    Pasta & vegetables : low-fat recipes-- that work! / Chris Gluck ; illustrations by John Molenaar ; wine selections by Edmund Osterland. -- 1st ed.
    p. cm.
    Includes bibliographical references and index.
    ISBN: 1-891004-02-6
    1. Low-fat diet--Recipes. 2. Cookery (Pasta) 3. Cookery (Vegetables) I. Molenaar, John.
II. Osterland, Edmund. III. Title. IV. Title: Pasta and vegetables.

TX809.M17G58 1998   641.8'22
                                      QBI98-981

LCCN: 98-091496
Printed in USA

98 99 00 01 02 ♦ 10 9 8 7 6 5 4 3 2 1

Dedicated To

Arlyn Hackett

*Good friend, respected colleague and a true pioneer
in the field of healthy gourmet cooking.*

Table of Contents

"Pasta's on!"

A Pasta & Vegetable Fairy Tale

Once upon a time, a long, long time ago, pasta was funny-shaped spaghetti that came out of a can, and vegetables were something your mother forced you to eat before you could have dessert.

Boy, have times changed!

Dear Fellow Vegetable Lover

During our years of selling fresh pasta at southern California farmers' markets (see next page), my family and I developed a love for pasta and vegetables. Considering our easy access to every conceivable type of vegetable and our obvious access to pasta, combining the two was a natural. As a result, what started simply as a convenient way to use market leftovers, quickly turned into one of our favorite meals. It helped, of course, that the markets were a melting pot of recipe ideas; sometimes from farmers eager to share the "best" way to prepare their specialty crop, sometimes from regular customers proud to share a family favorite. More often than not, however, "recipes" were nothing more than spur-of-the-moment creations.

After all, what could be easier and tastier than pasta and vegetables? Whether it was just a simple summertime sauce of tomatoes, garlic and basil (page 38), a perfectly orchestrated Asian-style stir-fry (page 56), or a last-minute, haphazard conglomeration of seasonal left-overs (page 72), there was never a shortage of possibilities. It didn't take long for us to appreciate this versatility—especially with our hectic schedules.

Then, when we added to this versatility the many health benefits attributed to a diet high in vegetables and pasta, it only increased our passion for the combination—and when we began losing weight, it fueled it even more.

During the ensuing years, we collected scores of pasta recipes for our magazine, *Pasta Press*—some strictly vegetarian, some not. All, however, had the same criteria in three key areas: they had to taste great; they had to be relatively easy to make; and they had to be under 20% of calories from fat.

This book is a collection of some of the most popular vegetarian recipes from those years—including some with non-vegetarian options. They were developed in collaboration with ten of the finest chefs, cookbook authors and cooking instructors in America. So, whether you're a fellow vegetable lover, or it's just healthy, flavorful food that you're after, look no further! I'm sure you'll enjoy making these recipes as much as we enjoyed putting them together for you!

Introduction: How We Lost 20 Pounds Eating Pasta

It all started in April 1993. Our oldest daughter Erica, seven years old at the time, was so eager to earn her own spending money that she threatened to sell her Teddy bears on the sidewalk unless we could help her find a job. My wife, Mary, contacted several small businesses in our neighborhood on her behalf, but after being turned down for *any* type of employment, Erica realized that her only option was to start her own business. Being self-employed all our lives, Mary and I certainly didn't want to quash any entrepreneurial tendencies in our first-born—although we did have a few reservations about her youth!

For years we had purchased the most wonderful, homemade fresh pasta from a small neighborhood shop that specialized in exotically flavored pastas. Erica reasoned, with typical child-like innocence, that if she liked it so much everyone else would, too. So it came as no surprise when she proposed the idea of selling flavored fresh pasta at our local farmers' market one night a week. More to encourage her than anything else, we half-heartedly decided to give it a try. We started with $100 in product inventory and a few borrowed card tables and coolers.

Quite frankly, we never expected this venture to be anything more than a glorified lemonade stand—and we certainly didn't expect it to last for more than a couple of weeks. Were we ever in for a big surprise! The business quickly exploded. Eventually we had to give up our "real" jobs just to keep up with it.

Our enthusiasm was short-lived, however. While initial demand had been promising, sales began to decline as the novelty wore off. We learned the hard way that consumer awareness about flavored fresh pasta was practically non-existent. Many of our regular customers didn't know how to prepare it correctly, nor did they realize its enormous versatility.

So, we set out to educate our customers by writing a simple one-page brochure, *Commonly Asked Questions About Flavored Fresh Pasta.* In it we shared some basic cooking techniques and explained how to create delicious, easy-to-prepare low-fat sauces. Response was enthusiastic, and sales picked up again. Mission accomplished!

But it didn't stop there. After discovering how delicious pasta could really be, many of our now-devoted, regular customers encouraged us to print a new brochure with even more tips and recipes. Over the course of the following year, the one-page brochure evolved into a small, locally distributed newsletter; then into our internationally distributed quarterly magazine, *Pasta Press*; and ultimately, this series of books.

That original brochure also explained how we effortlessly lost 20 pounds each by switching to a low-fat diet utilizing lots of pasta. This is an important point— and the one that ultimately brought about the magazine and then these books. You see, ***our weight loss happened quite by accident.***

Like many Americans, we were struggling to lose those last few extra pounds. We'd go on a diet, lose them, get bored, go off the diet, and then gain them, and a few more, right back again. It seemed that no matter how hard we tried, we were doomed to failure. To make matters worse, every time we thought we had everything under control, our taste buds would stage their own little revolution, saying "We don't care how healthy this is! It tastes terrible and we're not going to eat it anymore!"

But what happened next was quite unexpected. One day about three months after starting the business, Mary and I realized that our clothes were fitting more loosely. This came as a real shock since one of the fringe benefits of working at a farmers' market is that there's never any shortage of food. As a result, and because we were never ones to push aside our plates, we found that we were eating larger and larger quantities of food. If anything, we should have expected to gain weight. Stepping on the scale however, confirmed our hopeful suspicions. ***We had each lost 20 pounds—all while consuming greater quantities of food than ever before, <u>and</u> without offending our temperamental taste buds! Further-more, we both had more energy than ever and, as another unexpected bonus, a subsequent check-up revealed that our cholesterol levels were in the 140's!***

Ecstatic, we wanted to share the good news with everyone. So we threw ourselves into learning everything we could about how pasta related to healthful and delicious eating. Along the way we discovered overwhelming clinical evidence indicating that a diet low in fats, especially saturated fats, and high in complex carbohydrates and fiber will produce the welcome benefits we experienced. Since pasta is high in complex carbohydrates, and because our sauces had typically been spur-of-the-moment low-fat concoctions based largely on left-over produce from the farmers' markets, it gradually dawned on us that ***we had unknowingly developed healthful eating habits!*** In retrospect, what made it so easy was that the food tasted good—and there was plenty of it.

It didn't take us long to realize that our new high-complex carbohydrate, high-fiber, low-fat eating regimen had painlessly accomplished what a lifetime of deprivation-based dieting never would. So, if you're interested in losing weight or improving your health—or if you just want to sample some great new pasta dishes, I invite you to try the recipes that follow. They're all under 20% of calories from fat and I'm confident your taste buds will approve. Our favorite complement is, "How can this be low-fat? It tastes too good to be healthy!"

One final note: This is what worked for us and for countless others. However, I am not a doctor nor am I dispensing medical advice. Please check with your personal physician and do your own independent research before making any dietary, exercise or lifestyle changes.

To your good health and long life!

Why are the Recipes Under 20% of Calories from Fat?

Dieting...Without Going Hungry!

Ask any dieter why it's difficult to stick with most diets and the likely response will be one word—deprivation! Typically, most conventional weight loss diets are based on caloric restriction of some type, and most of us simply don't enjoy being restricted or deprived—especially when it comes to food! If we leave the table even the least bit hungry, that's a sure sign of temptations to come! Herein is where I believe the problem lies. Even though the average dieter will probably experience some degree of immediate weight loss on most diets, for many this may simply not be enough to combat the persistent hunger pangs typically associated with deprivation-based dieting. That's the bad news. Now here's the good news.

How Does Pasta Fit In?

Many studies (and our personal experiences) indicate that by implementing a low-fat, high-complex carbohydrate diet, weight loss may be achieved without deprivation. Although the USDA currently defines a low-fat diet as one that derives less than 30% of its calories from fat, many physicians and nutritionists recommend levels below 20%. This latter criteria is the one our family uses and the one that all of the recipes in this book follow.

If your objective is to make the switch to low-fat eating, pasta may be just what you're looking for. Because it is high in complex carbohydrates, and because the fat calories comprise less than 10% of total calories, by itself, pasta immediately satisfies the under 20% criteria. And, because it is an extremely versatile base to which you can add a multitude of your favorite ingredients, it can also be prepared in ways to satisfy just about everyone's taste bud criteria. Beware of rich sauces containing extravagant amounts of cheese, cream, butter and meats, though! They can quickly push the overall percentage of calories from fat to unacceptably high levels.

Exactly what is it about eating low-fat, high-fiber, high-complex carbohydrate foods that enables most people to eat until they're satisfied—with apparent disregard to calorie counting? To illustrate let's first discuss the differences between calories.

Are All Calories Created Equal?

In a word, no! Calories from fat and calories from carbohydrates or protein differ in two very important ways. First, one gram of fat has over twice as many calories as an identical amount of either carbohydrates or protein. (1 gram of fat = 9 calories vs. 1 gram of carbohydrates or protein = 4 calories.) Second, it is much easier for our bodies to convert foods that are high in fat directly into body fat than it is to convert foods that are high in carbohydrates.

What does this mean? The body's ability to store complex carbohydrates like pasta is limited. This is in direct contrast to its ability to store fat calories—which have a tendency to go straight to our hips or belly! Even when people eat more complex carbohydrates than their bodies can absorb, these excess calories are more readily burned than excess calories from fat. Put another way, you will have to work much harder to burn off a high-fat cheeseburger than you will a low-fat serving of pasta—even though both may contain the identical amount of calories. Furthermore, the pasta portion will be much larger than the cheeseburger—meaning that you will most likely get filled up on fewer calories. This suggests that perhaps the *composition* of one's diet may be of great importance when it comes to gaining or losing weight.

Overeating High-Fat Foods is Easier

As a practical matter, it's much easier to overeat high-fat foods than it is low-fat foods. For example, did you know that a 1½ ounce portion of potato chips has the same amount of calories as a 10 ounce baked potato? Even though the *amount* of calories is identical, you'll probably still be hungry after eating the chips (and want to eat a lot more)! On the other hand, you'll probably feel full after eating the baked potato. But here's the real problem: The chips have over 14 grams of fat while the baked potato has less than ½ gram.

Here's another example. Compare the recipes in this book against a cheeseburger, fries and a shake—a typical fast food meal. The pasta recipes average around 465 calories, with calories from fat averaging less than 16%. However, depending on the restaurant, the fast food meal will average around 1,600 calories with almost 50% of those coming from fat. Furthermore, most of the pasta recipe's fat is monounsaturated, or "good" fat, while much of the fast food meal's is saturated, artery clogging, "bad" fat.

From strictly a caloric standpoint, you would have to eat over three main course servings of pasta to equal the number of calories in one fast food meal. Is it possible? Yes. Is it likely? Probably not.

For the sake of argument, let's assume that you did "overeat" low-fat (less than 20% of calories from fat) complex carbohydrate foods like pasta. Would you gain weight? Maybe, maybe not. Let's take a look at a recent study done at the University of Illinois at Chicago.

An Actual Case Study

In a well-documented study (*American Journal of Clinical Nutrition, Vol. 54, pp. 304–310, 1991*) researchers from UIC performed a 24 week study on 18 overweight sedentary women. The subjects were fed a control diet of 37% fat (the average American's diet) for an initial 4 week period and then switched to a 20% fat diet. All other factors, including lack of exercise, were constantly monitored and remained stable throughout the study. After 20 weeks of lower-fat eating, the women lost an average of approximately 5 pounds each—*in spite of consuming significantly more (15–28%) calories than on the high-fat diets.*

Dr. Phyllis Bowen, one of the original researchers, told me that many of the women complained that they couldn't eat all of their food when the initial switch was made from high-fat to low-fat—*even though the calorie levels were the same!* It took them 1–2 weeks to adjust to the higher quantities of lower-fat food. Dr. Bowen went on to say that after this adjustment period, they had to gradually increase the quantity of food in an attempt to maintain body weight. ***Despite these efforts, the group as a whole continued to lose weight!***

But perhaps most importantly, everyone's *lean muscle mass percentage* increased while their body fat decreased. Muscle weighs more than fat but takes up less volume. In addition to countless health benefits, a higher percentage of lean muscle mass usually translates to a more attractive physique. So by definition, in addition to just losing weight, these women were also reshaping. Dr. Bowen confirmed this, saying that even though the average weight loss was *only* five pounds, many of the women were ecstatic at being able to fit back into clothes they hadn't been able to wear in years!

The Bottom Line

Whether you are interested in weight management, maintaining your health, or just great food, we have seen many benefits to a low-fat, yet savory eating regimen that includes lots of complex carbohydrates like pasta. As they have for us, I hope these recipes help you achieve your weight and health goals. I think you'll be thrilled with the long term results!

Who's in the Kitchen?

William Anatooskin William Anatooskin is the author of *From Uncle Bill's Kitchen* (Bilkin Enterprises Ltd), a collection of old Russian, Ukrainian and other ethnic favorites, plus some modern West Coast favorites.
- *Lemon Broccoli Penne (page 54)*

Hugh Carpenter Hugh Carpenter is cookbook author, cooking instructor and proprietor of Camp Napa Culinary, a cooking school in Napa Valley. Known for creative recipes with explosive flavors, his current "Hot" cookbook series (*Hot Wok, Hot Pasta, Hot Barbecue, etc.,* Ten Speed Press) is breaking all records.
- *Mushroom & Red Wine Sauce (page 66)*
- *Pasta with Roasted Tomato Salsa (page 70)*

Stella Fong Stella Fong is a research biologist turned cooking instructor. Her scientific understanding of food, coupled with her personal love of cooking, has enabled her to develop a unique style equally popular among children and adults.
- *Asian-Style Roasted Eggplant Sauce (page 82)*

Frank Garofolo Frank Garofolo, whose specialty is Italian cuisine, caters and teaches cooking classes throughout the Northeast.
- *Artichoke & White Wine Sauce (page 62)*

Chris Gluck Chris Gluck is a cooking instructor, the author of this book and its companion, *Pasta & Garlic,* and the publisher/editor of *Pasta Press* magazine. His mission is to show everyone that, with pasta, it's easy to eat delicious and healthy food at the same time.
- *Southwest Pasta Salad (page 22)*
- *Tropical Fruit Pasta Salad (page 26)*
- *Vegetarian Chili Pasta (page 32)*
- *"Got-To-Go" Minestrone (page 34)*
- *Tomato & Garlic Raw Sauce...with a Salsa Variation (page 38)*
- *Basic Marinara Sauce...with Variations (page 40)*
- *Creamy Tomato Blender Sauce (page 44)*
- *Pan-Roasted Garlic Chunks with Tomatoes & Arugula (page 50)*
- *Asian Vegetable Stir-Fry with Ginger & Lime (page 56)*
- *Caramelized Sweet Onion Sauce (page 58)*
- *Orzo Vegetable Melange (page 64)*
- *Grilled Vegetable Medley with Pasta (page 72)*
- *Roasted Red Bell Pepper Pesto (page 74)*
- *Roasted Squash Sauce with Ginger & Sherry (page 80)*

Arlyn Hackett Arlyn Hackett is a cooking instructor and the consulting editor of *Pasta Press*. He served as the executive chef at *Pritikin Longevity Center* for seven years and was also the star of the PBS television cooking series, *Health Smart Gourmet Cooking*. He is the author of several low-fat cookbooks.
- *Orzo Waldorf Salad with a Cider Vinaigrette (page 28)*
- *Salsa Cruda Italiana (page 42)*
- *French Tomato Sauce (page 46)*
- *Moroccan Roasted Pepper Pasta Sauce (page 78)*

Jeanne Jones Jeanne Jones is the syndicated columnist of *Cook It Light* and the author of numerous low-fat cookbooks. Her message of common sense and moderation speaks directly to the health concerns of today, proving once again that eating well does not mean sacrificing the pleasures and enjoyment of food.
- *Ginger Pasta Appetizer (page 30)*

Patrick Lambert Trained in Switzerland, Patrick Lambert is the executive chef of Doc Martin's Restaurant at the Taos Inn in New Mexico. A leader in the field of healthful cooking, he replaces traditional sauces made with heavy cream and butter with highly flavored, low-fat purees, reductions and broths.
- *Mediterranean Pasta Salad (page 24)*

Daniel McKenna Voted Rising Star Chef of the Year by the San Francisco Chronicle, Daniel McKenna received his formal training at the California Culinary Academy. He has worked in many prestigious restaurants and hotels.
- *Twice-Cooked Penne in a Carrot Reduction (page 60)*

Grady Spears Known for his "cowboy cuisine," a unique cooking style that bridges the gap between Southwestern and Tex-Mex, Grady Spears in the chef and co-owner of the *Reata* restaurants in Fort Worth and Alpine (Texas).
- *Texas Tomato Cream Sauce (page 48)*

Adelina Willem Adelina Willem is the author and publisher of *Because Life is Too Short for Plain Noodles* and the founder of *Adelina's Products*, a specialty manufacturer of flavored pastas.
- *Fire-Roasted New Mexico Pepper Sauce (page 76)*

◆ ◆ ◆ ◆ ◆

Edmund Osterland, MS Edmund Osterland is the wine editor of *Pasta Press* magazine. He is the first American ever to pass the grueling Master Sommelier exam—recognized by many as the most difficult wine tasting exam in the world. He teaches wine education and appreciation courses and serves as a consultant to the industry. His special area of expertise is on pairing wine and food for maximum flavor synergism.
- *All Wine Picks*

The 10 Commandments for Preparing Perfect Pasta

I.   Thou shalt not answer thy telephone while cooking pasta.

You will jeopardize commandment #VII.

II.   Thou shalt cook thy pasta in a large pot.

Your pasta will cook evenly and taste better if cooked in lots of water. Use at least 6 quarts of water (in an 8 quart pot) per pound of pasta.

III.   Thou shalt always start with cold water.

Starting with cold water ensures that your pasta won't pick up any "off" tastes from your hot water heater.

IV.   Thou shalt cook thy pasta in rapidly boiling water.

Your pasta will get mushy otherwise.

V.   Thou shalt salt thy pasta water.

Pasta cooked in unsalted water tastes bland. Use 1–2 tablespoons of salt per gallon of water.

VI.   Thou shalt frequently stir thy pasta while cooking.

Your pasta will cook evenly and won't stick together if stirred at regular intervals.

VII. Thou shalt not overcook thy pasta.

Overcooked pasta tastes mushy, lacks flavor and texture, and falls apart. Pasta should be cooked "al dente," or "to the tooth," meaning that it's tender but still firm.

VIII. Thou shalt not time thy pasta.

Listed cooking times are approximate. There are too many variables that make timing virtually impossible to do accurately and consistently. Instead, frequently test your pasta for doneness by biting into a strand during the last minutes of cooking. When it's "al dente," drain immediately.

IX. Thou shalt prepare thy sauce before cooking thy pasta.

Cooked pasta waits for no one! Always make sure your sauce is ready (or will be ready) the moment your pasta is done. Adding it to the pasta immediately ensures that your pasta won't stick together in a hopeless clump. Once sauced, serve immediately!

X. Thou shalt not rinse thy pasta after cooking.

Rinsing pasta removes some of its starch. This small amount of starch thickens the sauce and helps it cling to the pasta better. The three exceptions are: 1) If the pasta is going to be used in a cold pasta salad, or 2) If the pasta is going to be used in a baked dish (like lasagne) or in a hot soup (like minestrone), or 3) If you accidentally overcooked the pasta (probably as a result of not heeding commandment #I) and need to stop the cooking process in a hurry.

Soups and Salads

PASTA salads have come a long way since the days of the ubiquitous mayonnaise-laden macaroni salad still served in most corner delis and school lunch rooms. Thankfully, there are now hundreds of options, with more creative and delicious new recipes cropping up daily. If you're ready for a refreshing, more healthful change of pace, this sampling of pasta salads might be just what you're looking for.

Here's a spicy Southwest salad with a delightfully peppery punch; a rich-tasting Mediterranean salad complete with the requisite Greek olives, Feta cheese and sun-dried tomatoes; an unusual tropical fruit salad with a delicious fat-free pureed mango sauce; a zesty spin on grandma's traditional Waldorf salad; and even a tangy Asian-style ginger flavored appetizer/salad. All can be made well in advance and are equally suited for picnics, casual entertaining or even fine dining.

Of course, if it's heartier fare you're after, try making a big kettle of soup or chili. You can clean out your refrigerator while throwing together a pot of "got-to-go" minestrone, or please even die-hard carnivores with a steaming bowl of vegetarian chili—complete with all the "fixin's."

Southwest Pasta Salad

Serves 8–12

Flavor combinations typical of the Southwest blend to create this refreshingly spicy and easy-to-make dish. You can adjust the spiciness to suit your palate simply by varying the amount of cayenne.

Pasta
fusilli or spiral-shaped pasta of your choice
(1 pound dried or 1¼ pounds fresh)

Dressing
4 teaspoons chili powder

½–1½ teaspoons cayenne (½ is mildly spicy, 1½ is hot)

1 teaspoon ground cumin

1½ teaspoons finely ground black pepper

½ teaspoon salt

½ teaspoon garlic powder

1 teaspoon dried oregano, crushed

3½ tablespoons red wine vinegar

¼ cup fresh squeezed lime juice

1½ tablespoons canola oil

1 tablespoon honey

Vegetables
1 (16 oz.) package frozen sweet corn kernels, thawed

2 (15 oz.) cans black beans, drained and rinsed

1 red bell pepper, finely diced

¼ red onion, finely diced

3 green onions (both white and green parts), thinly sliced

½ bunch fresh cilantro, finely chopped

Advance Preparation: *30 minutes*
Combine all dressing ingredients in a bowl. Mix thoroughly, cover and set aside. Prepare vegetables as specified. ***Ingredients may be prepared <u>up to 8 hours in advance</u> if refrigerated.***

WINE PICKS
WHITE .... *Fumé Blanc*
RED .... *Valpolicella*

22

Final Preparation: *15 minutes*

1. Cook pasta in plenty of rapidly boiling salted water until *al dente*. Drain and place in an extra-large serving bowl. Add all vegetables in succession, tossing thoroughly between each addition.

2. Drizzle with dressing and toss thoroughly to evenly coat ingredients. Serve immediately while still warm, or allow to cool and serve at room temperature. (See **Cooling Pasta for Salads** in *Basic Techniques Appendix*.) Refrigerate leftovers and allow to slowly warm to room temperature before serving again.

Chris Gluck

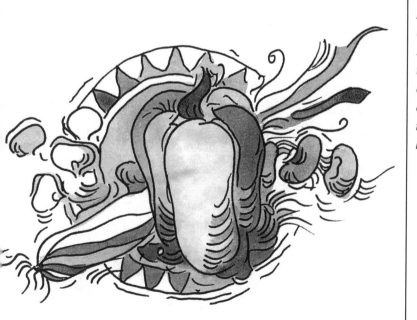

Mediterranean Pasta Salad

Serves 4

Pasta
farfalle, fusilli or pasta shape of your choice (¾ pound dried or 1 pound fresh)

Sauce
4 teaspoons olive oil (divided use)

1 tablespoon garlic, minced

1 red onion, quartered and sliced

¼ pound snow peas, ends trimmed

½ pound asparagus, bias cut into 1" pieces

2 ounces sun-dried tomatoes (not oil-packed), re-hydrated in hot water and julienned (See Glossary)

3 tablespoons balsamic vinegar

1 red bell pepper, diced

¼ cup Kalamata (Greek) olives (or oil-cured black olives), pitted and coarsely chopped (See Glossary)

1½ ounces Feta cheese, crumbled (See Glossary)

salt and pepper, to taste

Advance Preparation: *30 minutes*
Prepare vegetables as specified. Re-hydrate sun-dried tomatoes in hot water for 10 minutes, or until soft. Drain, then slice re-hydrated tomatoes into julienne strips. Pit and chop olives. Crumble Feta. ***Ingredients may be prepared <u>up to 24 hours in advance</u> if refrigerated.***

Final Preparation: *15 minutes*
1. Heat 2 teaspoons olive oil in a large skillet or stir-fry pan over medium-high heat. Add garlic and sauté

30 seconds. Immediately add onion, snow peas, asparagus and sun-dried tomatoes. Sauté 3–5 minutes, stirring constantly. Deglaze skillet with balsamic vinegar and reduce until almost evaporated, about 1 minute. Remove from heat and allow to cool to room temperature.

2. Meanwhile, cook pasta in plenty of rapidly boiling salted water until *al dente*. Drain and immediately toss with remaining 2 teaspoons olive oil. Add cooled vegetable mixture and red bell pepper and toss again. Add olives and Feta and toss once more. Season to taste with salt and pepper. Serve immediately while still warm, or allow to cool and serve at room temperature. (See **Cooling Pasta for Salads** in *Basic Techniques Appendix*.) Refrigerate leftovers and allow to slowly warm to room temperature before serving again.

Patrick Lambert

Nutrition Data
(per serving)

Calories: **499**

Calories from Fat: **19.2%**

Total Fat: **10.8 g**

Saturated Fat: **2.7 g**

Cholesterol: **9 mg**

Sodium: **424 mg**

Carbohydrates: **84 g**

Dietary Fiber: **8.1 g**

Protein: **18 g**

Tropical Fruit Pasta Salad

Serves 6–8

Pasta
farfalle or pasta shape of your choice (½ pound dried)
2 teaspoons canola oil

Sauce
1 mango, peeled and pitted
3 tablespoons lime juice
1½ teaspoons ginger root, grated (See Glossary)
1 tablespoon honey
3 tablespoons apple cider

Fruits *(See **Tips** for substitutions and alternatives.)*
1 cup fresh pineapple, cut into bite-sized chunks
1 cup seedless grapes
1 cup cantaloupe balls
1 pear, cored and cut into small bite-sized pieces
1 cup tangerine sections
¼ cup fresh mint leaves, chiffonade (See Glossary)

Advance Preparation: *30 minutes plus chilling time*
   Cook pasta in plenty of rapidly boiling <u>un</u>salted water until *al dente*. Drain, rinse with cold water and drain thoroughly again. Place in a large mixing bowl and toss with canola oil. Refrigerate until chilled. Puree all sauce ingredients in a blender until smooth. Refrigerate until chilled. ***Ingredients may be prepared <u>up to 8 hours in advance</u> if refrigerated.***

Final Preparation: *20 minutes plus chilling time*
   1. Prepare fruits as specified.

2. Drizzle chilled mango sauce over chilled pasta. Toss until thoroughly coated. Add fruits and toss until evenly distributed. Sprinkle in mint and toss until evenly distributed. Cover and refrigerate until chilled, about 3 hours.

Chris Gluck

NUTRITION DATA
(per serving)

Calories: **229**

Calories from Fat: **9.0%**

Total Fat: **2.4 g**

Saturated Fat: **0.3 g**

Cholesterol: **0 mg**

Sodium: **8 mg**

Carbohydrates: **49 g**

Dietary Fiber: **3.3 g**

Protein: **5 g**

Orzo Waldorf Salad with Cider Vinaigrette

Serves 8

A typical Waldorf salad contains about 40 grams of fat and 30 mg of cholesterol per serving. Contrast that with the less than 5 grams of fat and zero mg of cholesterol in this pasta salad variation. Next time you don't want to get filled up before the main course arrives, try this lighter and more refreshing version instead!

Pasta
orzo (1½ cups dried)

Salad
2½ cups apple cider (See **Tips**)
1 apple, cored and finely diced
1 cup seedless grapes, halved
½ cup celery, finely diced
¼ cup walnuts, very coarsely chopped
1 head butter lettuce

Vinaigrette
2/3 cup apple cider (See **Tips**)
3 tablespoons fresh squeezed lime juice
1 tablespoon finely grated lime zest (See **Zesting Citrus Fruits** in Basic Techniques Appendix)
1 tablespoon canola oil
1 tablespoon fresh basil, chiffonade (See Glossary)
1 tablespoon fresh mint, chiffonade (See Glossary)

Advance Preparation: *45 minutes plus chilling time*
Heat cider in a large saucepan. When hot, reduce heat to low and add orzo. Stir constantly until orzo absorbs cider, about 10–12 minutes. (See **Cooking Perfect Orzo** in *Basic Techniques Appendix*.) Turn off heat, cover pan and wait 10 minutes. After 10 minutes remove orzo and spread on dinner plates to cool. Refrigerate until cold, about 3 hours. Prepare grapes, celery and walnuts as specified. Dice apple at the last minute to prevent discoloration. Combine all

WINE PICKS
WHITE ......*German Riesling*
RED............................. *N/A*

vinaigrette ingredients and whisk together until thoroughly blended. ***Orzo may be cooked <u>up to 1 day in advance</u> if refrigerated. Salad ingredients, except apple, may be prepared <u>up to 8 hours in advance</u> if refrigerated. Vinaigrette may be prepared <u>up to 1 week in advance</u> if refrigerated.***

Final Preparation: *5 minutes*

1. Combine chilled orzo with all remaining salad ingredients except lettuce. Add vinaigrette and toss thoroughly, using your fingers to break up any stubborn orzo clumps.

2. To serve, line individual salad plates with lettuce leaves and top with a scoop of orzo.

Arlyn Hackett

TIPS, HINTS & SHORT-CUTS

Many local apple growers press their fruit into unfiltered raw cider. If you're fortunate enough to live near such an apple growing region, try it in this recipe. It will add even more zip to this already "zippy" dish. Look for raw cider at farmers' markets and specialty stores. It is a perishable product that lasts about a week in the refrigerator or about 6 months in the freezer.

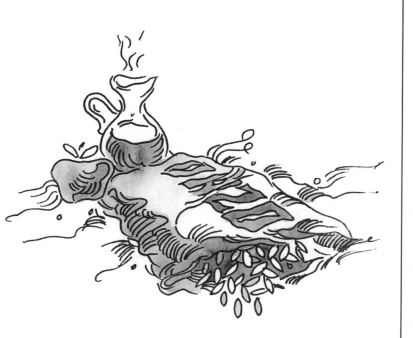

NUTRITION DATA
(per serving)

Calories: **244**
Calories from Fat: **17.3%**
Total Fat: **4.9 g**
Saturated Fat: **0.4 g**
Cholesterol: **0 mg**
Sodium: **16 mg**
Carbohydrates: **46 g**
Dietary Fiber: **2.7 g**
Protein: **7 g**

Ginger Pasta Appetizer

Serves 4 as an Appetizer

This quick Asian-style appetizer can be prepared in about the same amount of time it takes the pasta water to boil. Its spicy ginger flavor instantly excites the palate— making it a great way to start any meal!

Pasta
angel hair or spaghettini (½ pound dried or fresh)

Sauce
¼ cup rice vinegar (See Glossary)

2 tablespoons soy sauce

2 tablespoons honey

1 teaspoon Chinese chili paste (See Glossary), or red pepper flakes

2 tablespoons ginger root, minced (See Glossary)

2 green onions (both white and green parts), finely sliced

2 teaspoons dark sesame oil (See Glossary)

Advance Preparation: *10 minutes*

Prepare ginger and green onions as specified. Combine all sauce ingredients except sesame oil and whisk together until thoroughly blended. **Sauce may be prepared <u>up to 2 days in advance</u> if refrigerated.**

Final Preparation: *10 minutes*

1. Cook pasta in plenty of rapidly boiling salted water until *al dente*. Drain and toss with sesame oil. Add sauce mixture, toss gently and serve immediately.

Jeanne Jones

WINE PICKS
WHITE ....*Riesling*
RED.....................*Pinot Noir*

30

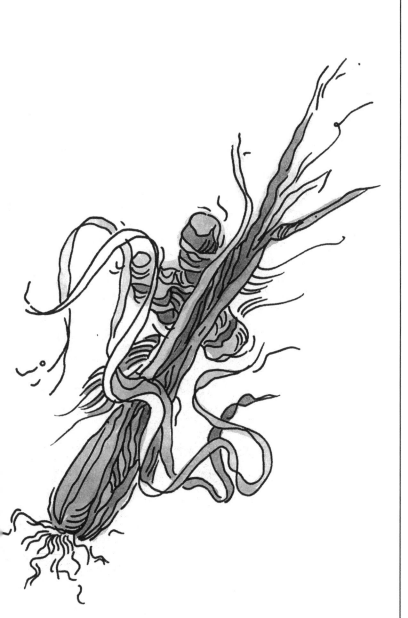

TIPS, HINTS & SHORT-CUTS

This tangy appetizer easily doubles as a cold pasta salad. Or, with the addition of bite-size pieces of cooked seafood or poultry, it turns into a more substantial non-vegetarian entree.

NUTRITION DATA
(per serving)

Calories: **295**
Calories from Fat: **10.0%**
Total Fat: **3.4 g**
Saturated Fat: **0.5 g**
Cholesterol: **0 mg**
Sodium: **431 mg**
Carbohydrates: **59 g**
Dietary Fiber: **3.5 g**
Protein: **9 g**

Vegetarian Chili Pasta

Serves 12–16

Eggplant is the "meaty" non-meat secret ingredient that takes the place of beef in this hearty vegetarian chili. Don't be alarmed by the seemingly large amount specified— once cooked the eggplant reduces to a fraction of its uncooked size. This recipe may be halved if you'd prefer a smaller yield; however, leftovers easily keep 4–5 days in the refrigerator and, like most chilis, taste even better the next day.

Pasta
conchiglie or thick pasta shape(s)of your choice
   (½ pound dried)

Chili
4 tablespoons olive oil (divided use)
3 pounds eggplant, peeled and cut into ¾" thick slices
8 cloves garlic, minced
1 yellow onion, chopped
1 red bell pepper, chopped
4 zucchini, cut into ½" thick slices
1 (16 oz.) package frozen corn, thawed and rinsed
¾ cup chili powder
¼ cup ground cumin
3 (15 oz.) cans black beans, drained and rinsed
2 (28 oz.) cans diced tomatoes
1 (46 oz.) can tomato juice
your favorite bottled hot sauce (optional)
1 cup part skim milk mozzarella, grated
1 bunch green onions, thinly sliced
½ bunch fresh cilantro, minced

Advance Preparation: *1 hour (30 minutes of work)*
   Leach bitterness from eggplant. (See ***Eliminating Bitterness in Eggplant*** in *Basic Techniques Appendix*.) Cut eggplant slices into ¾" cubes. Prepare remaining vegetables as specified. ***Ingredients may be prepared <u>up to 8 hours in advance</u> if refrigerated.***

WINE PICKS
WHITE ..... *Sauvignon Blanc*
RED .... *Pinot Noir*

Final Preparation: *1¾ hours*

1. Heat 3 tablespoons olive oil in a large pot over high heat. Add eggplant cubes and cook 10 minutes, stirring almost constantly. Reduce heat to medium and cook another 10 minutes, stirring occasionally. Remove eggplant and reserve. (See **Tips**.)

2. Heat remaining 1 tablespoon olive oil in the same pot over high heat. Add garlic and stir-fry 30 seconds. Immediately add onion and bell pepper and cook 10 minutes, stirring frequently. Add zucchini and cook 10 minutes, stirring frequently. Add corn and cook 10 minutes, stirring frequently. Add reserved eggplant, chili powder, cumin, beans, tomatoes and tomato juice. Bring to a simmer, reduce heat to low and simmer 30 minutes, stirring occasionally.

3. Meanwhile, cook pasta in plenty of rapidly boiling salted water until *al dente*. Drain and rinse thoroughly with cold water.

4. After 30 minutes add cooked pasta to chili. Simmer 10 minutes longer, stirring occasionally. Season to taste with salt, pepper and/or bottled hot sauce if desired. Serve in large soup bowls, topping with cheese, green onions and cilantro at the table.

Chris Gluck

TIPS, HINTS & SHORT-CUTS

After cooking eggplant 20 minutes, some of it will stick to the pot. If you turn off the heat and leave the cooked eggplant in the pot for a few minutes, it will release some of its juices and automatically deglaze the pot, making removal a snap.

♦♦♦♦♦

If they're available, feel free to substitute fresh ingredients for the canned or frozen ones specified.

♦♦♦♦♦

Kidney or pinto beans may be substituted for the black beans. An equivalent amount of dried beans (follow package cooking instructions) may also be substituted.

NUTRITION DATA
(per serving)

Calories: **431**
Calories from Fat: **16.8%**
Total Fat: **8.6 g**
Saturated Fat: **1.7 g**
Cholesterol: **4 mg**
Sodium: **681 mg**
Carbohydrates: **75 g**
Dietary Fiber: **16.8 g**
Protein: **20 g**

"Got-To-Go" Minestrone

Serves 8–12

It all started one day while cleaning the refrigerator with my daughter, Erica. "These have got to go," I said, throwing a lonely leek, 3 slightly over-ripe tomatoes, and a wedge of cabbage on the counter.

"These have got to go, too," echoed Erica, adding 2 stalks of celery, a few carrots and some zucchini. Then it hit me. They didn't have to go. "Let's make 'got-to-go' minestrone instead!" I explained that minestrone is a traditional Italian soup containing vegetables, beans and pasta. Like most classic dishes, it has countless versions. The most fun way to make it, though, is without a recipe. Instead, you simply go through your refrigerator and put in whatever's "got to go!"

WINE PICKS
WHITE ....*Pinot Grigio*
RED........................ *Chianti*

Pasta
conchiglie or thick pasta shape(s)of your choice (½ pound dried)

Soup
1 tablespoon olive oil
6 cloves garlic, minced
1 onion, thinly sliced
1 leek, thinly sliced
2 celery stalks, cut into ¼" pieces
2 carrots, cut into ¼" slices
3 zucchini, cut into ¼" slices
¼ head cabbage, shredded
*2 quarts vegetable stock (See **Vegetable Stock Recipes** in Appendix)*
3 tomatoes, chopped, or 1 (14½ oz.) can diced tomatoes
1 tablespoon oregano, crushed
1 tablespoon basil, crushed
1 tablespoon rosemary, crushed
2 (15 oz.) cans kidney beans, drained and rinsed
½ cup freshly grated Parmesan

Advance Preparation: *30 minutes*
    Prepare vegetables as specified. ***Ingredients may be prepared <u>up to 24 hours in advance</u> if refrigerated.***

Final Preparation: *1¼ hours*

1. Heat olive oil in a large pot over medium-high heat. Add garlic and sauté 1 minute, stirring constantly. Immediately add onion, leek, celery and

carrots. Cook 5 minutes, stirring frequently. Add zucchini and cook 3 minutes, stirring frequently. Add cabbage and cook 3 minutes, stirring frequently. Add stock, tomatoes and herbs. Bring to a simmer, reduce heat to low and simmer 30 minutes, stirring occasionally.

2. Meanwhile, cook pasta in plenty of rapidly boiling salted water until *al dente*. Drain and rinse thoroughly with cold water.

3. After 30 minutes add cooked pasta and beans to soup. Simmer 10 minutes longer, stirring occasionally. Season to taste with salt and pepper if desired. Serve piping hot in large soup bowls, sprinkling Parmesan over each serving at the table.

Chris Gluck

TIPS, HINTS & SHORT-CUTS

Feel free to make substitutions and additions depending on what you have that's "got to go!" Some good options are: green beans, corn, peas, bell peppers (any color), different types of beans (home-cooked or canned), mushrooms (fresh or dried), potatoes, turnips, Italian parsley, different herbs of your choice (fresh or dried), tomato paste, tomato juice or even V-8® juice!

NUTRITION DATA
(per serving)

Calories: **265**
Calories from Fat: **12.4%**
Total Fat: **3.8 g**
Saturated Fat: **1.1 g**
Cholesterol: **3 mg**
Sodium: **222 mg**
Carbohydrates: **46 g**
Dietary Fiber: **8.0 g**
Protein: **14 g**

Tomato Sauces

WHETHER it was microwaved straight out of a jar, or lovingly prepared from scratch and simmered for hours, tomato sauce must be the most popular, or at least the most often prepared, pasta topping of all time. But tomato sauce is more than just the predictable marinara we've all enjoyed (or endured) over the years. Here's an eclectic collection of some of my favorites—including, of course, the king of all comfort food—an easy-to-make, delicious basic marinara.

Here's a simple raw sauce that can be made start-to-finish in about 15 minutes; the aforementioned marinara with more options and variations than instructions; another Italian-style raw sauce perfect for picnics or casual summer evenings; a creamy blender sauce made almost entirely from shelf-stable pantry ingredients; an intensely flavored French-style sauce that uses wine instead of oil as the cooking medium; a versatile Texas-style broth with unlimited variations; and my wife's summertime favorite—a quick-to-make, garlicky tomato concoction tangled with peppery arugula leaves.

Next time you want tomato sauce, but can't bear the "same-old, same-old," try one of these palate pleasers instead.

Tomato & Garlic Raw Sauce ...with a Salsa Variation

Serves 4

Pasta
*linguine, fettuccine or pasta of your choice
(¾ pound dried or 1 pound fresh)*

Sauce
2 Roma tomatoes, seeded and finely diced
½ teaspoon salt, or to taste
15–20 fresh basil leaves, chiffonade (See Glossary)
1½ tablespoons olive oil (divided use)
3–4 cloves raw garlic, minced
¼ cup freshly grated Parmesan

Advance Preparation: *10 minutes*

Prepare tomatoes and basil as specified. Place tomatoes in a small bowl. Salt to taste. Add basil and toss. Drizzle with ½ tablespoon olive oil, toss gently again, cover and set aside. ***Ingredients may be prepared up to 8 hours in advance if refrigerated.***

Final Preparation: *10 minutes*

1. Cook pasta in plenty of rapidly boiling salted water until *al dente*. Drain and place in a large serving bowl. Drizzle with remaining 1 tablespoon olive oil and toss to coat pasta. Add garlic and toss to distribute evenly. Add tomato mixture and toss again.

2. Serve immediately, sprinkling Parmesan over each serving at the table. — OR — Allow to cool to room temperature and serve as a pasta salad. (See ***Cooling Pasta for Salads*** in *Basic Techniques Appendix*.)

Salsa Variation

double tomatoes to 4

substitute ½ cup minced cilantro for basil

add 2 green onions, very thinly sliced

add juice from 1 lime

delete Parmesan (but keep salt, olive oil and garlic)

Make a salsa by combining all sauce ingredients. Cover and set aside. **Salsa may be prepared <u>up to 8 hours in advance</u> if refrigerated.** Toss cooked pasta with salsa. Serve hot or at room temperature as per step #2.

Chris Gluck

TIPS, HINTS & SHORT-CUTS

Create your own spur-of-the-moment salsa by adding or substituting ingredients. Try finely minced red onion, finely chopped celery, diced cucumber, minced bell pepper (your choice of colors), corn kernels, black beans, sliced black olives, finely minced jalapeño peppers—whatever!

NUTRITION DATA
(per serving)

*Calories: **401***

*Calories from Fat: **18.4%***

*Total Fat: **8.2 g***

*Saturated Fat: **1.9 g***

*Cholesterol: **4 mg***

*Sodium: **372 mg***

*Carbohydrates: **68 g***

*Dietary Fiber: **2.8 g***

*Protein: **14 g***

Basic Marinara Sauce ...with Variations

Serves 4

Here it is! Undoubtedly the easiest, simplest, most delicious basic tomato sauce you'll ever make!

Pasta

pasta of your choice (¾ pound dried or 1 pound fresh)

Sauce

1 tablespoon olive oil

6 cloves garlic, minced

*3 cups fresh ripe tomatoes (about 2 pounds), peeled and coarsely chopped, or 1 (28 oz.) can diced tomatoes (See **Tips**)*

1 tablespoon basil, crushed

salt and pepper, to taste

¼ cup freshly grated Parmesan

Advance Preparation: *10 minutes*

Peel and chop tomatoes, taking care to reserve any juices. (See ***Peeling Tomatoes*** in *Basic Techniques Appendix*.) Peel and mince garlic. ***Ingredients may be prepared <u>up to 8 hours in advance</u> if refrigerated.***

Final Preparation: *30 minutes (or longer)*

1. Heat olive oil in a saucepan over medium heat. Add garlic and sauté until golden brown.

2. Add tomatoes, with their juices, and basil. Bring to a simmer. Reduce heat to low and simmer at least 20 minutes, stirring occasionally. Sauce is ready when it thickens to your liking. This is strictly a matter of personal preference. Some like a more liquid, "runny" sauce; others prefer a thicker sauce. The longer it cooks, the thicker it becomes. Season to taste with salt and pepper if desired.

WINE PICKS

WHITE ....*Pinot Grigio*
RED......................... *Chianti*

3. Meanwhile, cook pasta in plenty of rapidly boiling salted water until *al dente*. Drain and place into a large pre-heated serving bowl. Pour sauce over, toss and serve immediately. Sprinkle Parmesan over each serving at the table.

Variations

The variations on this versatile recipe are endless. You can substitute different herbs for the basil; rosemary being one of my personal favorites. You can sauté fresh vegetables of your choice with the garlic. Take them out and add them back to the sauce once the tomatoes have cooked—or let them simmer with the tomatoes. You can deglaze *(See Glossary)* the sautéed garlic with stock or wine and then let it reduce with the tomatoes. Or, for a non-vegetarian entree, you can add cooked poultry, seafood or meat to sauce. The best variations, however, are always the ones you create with whatever's available. This is one sauce that's not particular—so don't be afraid to experiment.

Chris Gluck

NUTRITION DATA
(per serving)

*Calories: **406***
*Calories from Fat: **14.9%***
*Total Fat: **6.8 g***
*Saturated Fat: **1.7 g***
*Cholesterol: **4 mg***
*Sodium: **112 mg***
*Carbohydrates: **72 g***
*Dietary Fiber: **3.8 g***
*Protein: **15 g***

Salsa Cruda Italiana

Serves 4–6

Pasta
fusilli, penne or pasta shape of your choice
  (1 pound dried or 1¼ pounds fresh)

Salsa
2 cups fresh, ripe tomatoes, finely chopped

¼ cup red onion, finely diced

¼ cup green bell pepper, finely diced

¼ cup celery, finely diced

2 cloves garlic, minced

2 tablespoons capers, drained and rinsed (See Glossary)

2 tablespoons fresh basil, chiffonade (See Glossary)

1 tablespoon olive oil

1 tablespoon fresh squeezed lemon juice

*¼ teaspoon red pepper flakes (See **Tips**)*

¼ teaspoon finely ground black pepper

Advance Preparation: *30 minutes*
Prepare vegetables as specified. ***Ingredients may be prepared (or entire salsa can be mixed as per step #1 below) up to 8 hours in advance if refrigerated.***

Final Preparation: *45 minutes (15 minutes of work)*

1. Combine salsa ingredients in a bowl. Set aside 30 minutes at room temperature to let flavors blend.

2. Just before serving, cook pasta in plenty of rapidly boiling salted water until *al dente*. Drain and place in a large serving bowl.

3. While pasta cooks, warm salsa in a microwave oven 1–2 minutes only.

4. Toss warmed salsa with cooked pasta. Cover and let stand 2 minutes before serving.

Arlyn Hackett

NUTRITION DATA
(per serving)

Calories: **385**
Calories from Fat: **10.4%**
Total Fat: **4.4 g**
Saturated Fat: **0.6 g**
Cholesterol: **0 mg**
Sodium: **50 mg**
Carbohydrates: **73 g**
Dietary Fiber: **3.4 g**
Protein: **13 g**

Creamy Tomato Blender Sauce

Serves 4–6

Here's a simple, tasty, easy-to-make dish the entire family will love. If you have young children, use a spiral-shaped pasta like fusilli and serve in bowls instead of plates. Sprinkle on a little Parmesan, give them the biggest soup spoons you own, and stand back! Chances are they'll be asking for seconds in less than five minutes!

Pasta
linguine, fettuccine or pasta of your choice
(1 pound dried or 1¼ pounds fresh)

Sauce
2 tablespoons olive oil
3 tablespoons garlic, chopped into pea-sized chunks
¼ –½ teaspoon red pepper flakes (¼ is mild, ½ is spicy)
1 (28 oz.) can diced tomatoes
1½ tablespoons basil
1 teaspoon sugar
1 tablespoon cornstarch
1 cup non-fat milk
salt and pepper, to taste
½ cup freshly grated Parmesan
¼ cup Italian parsley, minced (optional)

Advance Preparation: *15 minutes*

Drain canned tomatoes, reserving tomatoes and juice separately. Mix cornstarch with 1 tablespoon juice until smooth. Stir cornstarch mixture back into remaining juice. Stir in milk and reserve. Chop garlic as specified. **Ingredients may be prepared <u>up to 8 hours in advance</u> if refrigerated.**

Final Preparation: *25 minutes*

1. Heat olive oil in a saucepan over high heat. Add garlic chunks and pepper flakes. Sauté, stirring constantly until garlic is dark golden brown but not burnt, about 1 minute. Immediately add drained

WINE PICKS
WHITE .... *Chardonnay*
RED .... *Merlot*

44

tomatoes and stir constantly until spattering stops, about 2 minutes. Reduce heat to low and add basil and sugar. Simmer, stirring occasionally, until tomato liquids evaporate, about 10 minutes.

2. While tomatoes simmer, heat reserved tomato juice mixture over low heat in another saucepan. Simmer 10 minutes, or until mixture thickens, stirring frequently.

3. Combine cooked tomatoes and thickened tomato juice mixture in a blender. Puree on high speed 2 minutes, or until silky smooth. Season to taste with salt and pepper if desired. Return puree to a saucepan and keep warm.

4. Meanwhile, cook pasta in plenty of rapidly boiling salted water until *al dente*. Drain and place in a large serving bowl. Pour sauce over, toss and serve immediately. Sprinkle Parmesan and parsley over each serving at the table.

Chris Gluck

NUTRITION DATA
(per serving)

Calories: **492**
Calories from Fat: **17.9%**
Total Fat: **9.8 g**
Saturated Fat: **2.6 g**
Cholesterol: **7 mg**
Sodium: **441 mg**
Carbohydrates: **83 g**
Dietary Fiber: **4.2 g**
Protein: **19 g**

French Tomato Sauce

Serves 4

This sauce from Provence reflects the lighter side of French cuisine. Rather than sautéing vegetables in butter, here they are sweated in a fat-free liquid. While obviously a great technique for the diet conscious, many French chefs routinely use this method simply because it's an effective way to intensify the natural flavor of vegetables—fat or no fat. Then, by blending a small amount of olive oil into the sauce at the last minute, these amplified flavors are almost instantly transported throughout the rest of the dish.

Pasta
linguine, fettuccine or pasta of your choice
   (¾ pound dried or 1 pound fresh)

Sauce
½ cup dry white wine (more if necessary)
1 cup red onion, finely diced
4 cloves garlic, minced
4 cups Roma tomatoes, diced
½ cup red bell pepper, finely diced
1 bay leaf
¼ teaspoon ground fennel seed
1/8 teaspoon ground nutmeg
¼ teaspoon cayenne pepper
12 black olives, pitted and chopped
2 tablespoons capers, drained and rinsed (See Glossary)
1 green onion (both white and green parts), finely chopped
1 tablespoon olive oil
1 tablespoon tomato paste, optional (See Glossary)
1 tablespoon fresh basil, minced
1 tablespoon Italian parsley, minced

Advance Preparation: 30 minutes
Prepare vegetables as specified. (Mince fresh herbs at the last minute.) **Ingredients may be prepared up to 8 hours in advance if refrigerated.**

Final Preparation: 45 minutes
1. Place wine, red onion and garlic into a large saucepan. Cover and cook on low 15 minutes.

WINE PICKS
WHITE ..... Sauvignon Blanc
RED .... Pinot Noir

2. Add tomatoes, bell pepper and dry spices. Cover and cook on low 20 minutes. Check periodically and add more wine if sauce becomes too dry.

3. Stir in olives, capers, green onion and olive oil. Cook, uncovered, 3 minutes, stirring frequently. Blend in tomato paste if a thicker sauce is desired. Stir in fresh herbs just before serving.

4. Meanwhile, cook pasta in plenty of rapidly boiling salted water until *al dente*. Drain and place into a large pre-heated serving bowl. Pour sauce over, toss and serve immediately.

Arlyn Hackett

TIPS, HINTS & SHORT-CUTS

For a non-vegetarian entree, poach scallops, shrimp or bite-sized chicken breast pieces in the sauce just before adding the fresh herbs at the end of step #3. Simmer a few minutes until done; then proceed with the recipe.

NUTRITION DATA
(per serving)

Calories: **461**
Calories from Fat: **14.1%**
Total Fat: **7.1 g**
Saturated Fat: **1.0 g**
Cholesterol: **0 mg**
Sodium: **189 mg**
Carbohydrates: **82 g**
Dietary Fiber: **6.5 g**
Protein: **14 g**

Texas Tomato Cream Sauce

Serves 6

The flavorful "Texas Tomato Broth" yields enough broth to make this recipe about three times. Although you can make less by scaling the broth ingredients back proportionately, it takes the same amount of time to make a triple batch or a single batch. Since it freezes well, you might as well make more and save the excess for a time when you need to put dinner on the table in a hurry. The broth can also be used as a base for many other sauces. Have fun experimenting on your own, or see **Tips** on the next page for some ideas.

Pasta
linguine, fettuccine or pasta of your choice
   (1 pound dried or 1¼ pounds fresh)

Texas Tomato Broth *(Yields 10± cups. See sidebar notes.)*
6 tablespoons garlic, minced

3 tablespoons thyme

1 teaspoon basil

2 teaspoons salt

1½ tablespoons ground black pepper

3 tablespoons balsamic vinegar

3 tablespoons olive oil

2½ cups red onions, thinly sliced

4 pounds Roma tomatoes, cut in half lengthwise

2½ tablespoons brown sugar

3 cups tomato juice

2 cups tomato puree

Sauce
3 cups Texas Tomato Broth (recipe follows)
¾ cup light cream (half & half)

Advance Preparation: *1½ hours (45 minutes of work)*
   Make the "Texas Tomato Broth" as follows:
Combine garlic, thyme, basil, salt, pepper, balsamic vinegar and olive oil. Toss mixture with onions until well-coated. Place in two 9" x 13" glass baking pans and spread evenly to edges. Place tomatoes (cut side up) on top of mixture. Bake at 325° until tomatoes wilt

WINE PICKS
WHITE .... *Chardonnay*
RED .... *Syrah*

and onions begin to caramelize, about 45–60 minutes. Scrape out onions and tomatoes and place into a blender. Add remaining broth ingredients and puree until smooth. This will need to be done in stages depending on the size of your blender. **Broth may be used immediately, or prepared <u>up to 4 days in advance</u> if refrigerated or <u>up to 2 months in advance</u> if frozen.**

Final Preparation: *15 minutes*

1. Combine cooled broth and cream in a saucepan. Heat on low until hot but not boiling, stirring frequently.

2. Meanwhile, cook pasta in plenty of rapidly boiling salted water until *al dente*. Drain and place in a large pre-heated serving bowl. Pour sauce over, toss and serve immediately.

Grady Spears

TIPS, HINTS & SHORT-CUTS

The "Texas Tomato Broth" can be used as a base for other recipes. Here are 2 non-vegetarian options that use chicken.

◆◆◆◆◆

Combine 3 cups broth, 2 cups fat-free chicken stock and 1 pound bite-size pieces of grilled chicken breast. Heat through and toss with 1 pound cooked pasta and ½ cup minced cilantro.

◆◆◆◆◆

Combine 4 cups broth, 1¼ cups tomato juice and ¾ pound bite-size pieces of grilled smoked chicken sausage. Heat through and toss with 1 pound cooked pasta and ½ cup minced cilantro.

NUTRITION DATA
(per serving)

Calories: **393**
Calories from Fat: **16.2%**
Total Fat: **7.2 g**
Saturated Fat: **2.7 g**
Cholesterol: **11 mg**
Sodium: **378 mg**
Carbohydrates: **71 g**
Dietary Fiber: **4.2 g**
Protein: **13 g**

Pan-Roasted Garlic Chunks with Tomatoes & Arugula

Serves 4–6

This is one of my favorite impromptu dishes during the summer months when arugula is plentiful. As the arugula threads its way through the pasta, its peppery flavor complements the sweetness of the pan-roasted garlic chunks and fresh tomatoes with spectacular results—for both eye and palate.

Pasta
linguine, spaghetti or pasta of your choice
(1 pound dried or 1¼ pounds fresh)

Sauce
2 tablespoons olive oil

½ cup garlic cloves, chopped into pea-size chunks

1 quart fresh tomatoes, roughly chopped (including skins, seeds and juices)

*1 cup vegetable stock (See **Vegetable Stock Recipes** in Appendix) or dry white wine*

*2 quarts arugula leaves, tightly packed (See **Tips**)*

½ cup freshly grated Parmesan

Advance Preparation: *15 minutes*

Prepare vegetables as specified. **Ingredients may be prepared <u>up to 8 hours in advance</u> if refrigerated.**

Final Preparation: *15 minutes*

1. Heat olive oil in a large stir-fry pan or pot over medium-high heat. Add garlic and stir-fry until dark golden brown but not burnt, about 1½ minutes. Immediately remove half the garlic and reserve. Immediately add tomatoes and stock (or wine) to remaining garlic. Reduce heat to medium and simmer until sauce thickens slightly, about 3–4 minutes.

2. Meanwhile, cook pasta in plenty of rapidly boiling salted water until *al dente*. Drain and add directly to sauce. Toss gently to coat pasta with sauce. Add arugula and toss again so arugula wilts and tangles into pasta strands. Add reserved garlic chunks and

WINE PICKS
WHITE ..... *Sauvignon Blanc*
RED.......................... *Syrah*

toss again. Reduce heat to low and heat through 2–3 minutes. Serve immediately straight from pan, sprinkling Parmesan over each serving at the table.

Chris Gluck

TIPS, HINTS & SHORT-CUTS

Arugula is a pleasantly bitter, peppery-flavored leafy vegetable resembling spinach leaves with scalloped edges. It's generally available from late spring to early autumn. If it's out of season or otherwise unavailable, substitute fresh spinach leaves or a 50/50 blend of watercress leaves and spinach.

♦♦♦♦♦

For a more substantial non-vegetarian entree, substitute chicken stock for the vegetable stock, and add bite-size pieces of grilled chicken breasts to the sauce at the end of step #1.

NUTRITION DATA
(per serving)

Calories: **481**
Calories from Fat: **18.6%**
Total Fat: **10.0 g**
Saturated Fat: **2.5 g**
Cholesterol: **6 mg**
Sodium: **196 mg**
Carbohydrates: **81 g**
Dietary Fiber: **4.1 g**
Protein: **18 g**

Stir-Fried Vegetables

C ONJURING up visions of airborne Asian-style vegetables exploding from scorching hot woks, stir-fries have become a mainstay in Western cooking. Although some of these recipes are not true stir-fries in the exact sense of the definition, most utilize the high heat cooking typical of this easy-to-master technique. Because ingredients are cooked so rapidly, and continually tossed in the process, stir-fries use very little oil. This, of course, directly translates to lower fat content and more healthful cooking—without sacrifice of flavor.

Here's a typical Asian-style vegetable stir-fry punctuated with the distinctive flavors of ginger and lime; a broccoli stir-fry deglazed with a delicious lemon-infused broth; a caramelized onion sauce made by sweating a whopping two pounds of sweet onions down to almost a glace; a vegetable stir-fry with a depth of sweetness from a simple carrot juice reduction; a light and refreshing lemony artichoke sauce; an intensely rich mushroom sauce made even richer with the addition of red wine; and a risotto-style orzo cooked in a melange of stir-fried vegetables.

Stir-fries also offer tremendous versatility. In most cases, substitutions may be made to take advantage of seasonal produce—or just to suit your fancy.

Lemon Broccoli Penne

Serves 4

Here's a quick, easy and flavorful broccoli dish sure to please even non-broccoli lovers! Boiled with the pasta during its final minute of cooking, the barely blanched broccoli is then tossed with a tasty medley of stir-fried vegetables in a lemon infused broth—magically creating a delicious new flavor combination.

Pasta
penne (½ pound dried)

Sauce
1 tablespoon olive oil

2 garlic cloves, minced

½ red onion, thinly sliced

3 cups mushrooms, sliced

1½ cups vegetable stock (See **Vegetable Stock Recipes** in Appendix)

2 large tomatoes, diced

1 teaspoon oregano, crushed

¼ –½ teaspoon red pepper flakes (to taste)

¾ teaspoon finely grated lemon zest (See **Zesting Citrus Fruits** in Basic Techniques Appendix)

1 bunch fresh spinach leaves, stems trimmed

4 cups broccoli florets

¼ cup freshly grated Parmesan

Advance Preparation: *30 minutes*
    Prepare vegetables as specified. Grate lemon zest. **Ingredients may be prepared up to 8 hours in advance if refrigerated.**

Final Preparation: *30 minutes*
    1. Heat olive oil in a large pot over high heat. Add garlic and sauté 30 seconds, stirring constantly. Immediately add onion and sauté 2 minutes, stirring constantly. Immediately add mushrooms and sauté 5 minutes, or until lightly browned, stirring constantly.

2. Deglaze pot with ½ cup stock. Add tomatoes, oregano, pepper flakes and remaining stock. Reduce heat to medium-low and simmer 10 minutes, stirring occasionally.

3. Stir in lemon zest and spinach. Cover and cook 2 minutes, or until spinach wilts.

4. Meanwhile, cook pasta in plenty of rapidly boiling salted water for 1 minute less than the specified cooking time. At this point, add broccoli directly to pasta and cook both together for the final minute.

5. Drain pasta and broccoli combination and add to sauce. Toss all ingredients together, season to taste with salt and pepper if desired, and heat through 1–2 minutes. Transfer to a large pre-heated serving bowl, or serve immediately straight from the pot, sprinkling Parmesan over each serving at the table.

William Anatooskin

Asian Vegetable Stir-Fry with Ginger & Lime

Serves 4–6

*Like most stir-fries, this dish goes together very quickly once the sauce is mixed and the vegetables are cut. For convenience and ease of last minute preparation, you can prep the ingredients well in advance, or simply use a pre-packaged vegetable mix. See **Tips** for more options and ideas.*

Pasta
linguine or spaghetti (¾ pound dried)

Oil Infusion
2 tablespoons garlic, minced

1–2 tablespoons ginger root, finely chopped
 (1 is mild, 2 is spicy—See Glossary and **Tips**)

3 tablespoons canola oil

Sauce
3 tablespoons soy sauce

2 tablespoons oyster sauce (See Glossary)

¾ teaspoon ground white pepper

1 tablespoon garlic, minced

2–3 teaspoons ginger root, grated
 (2 is mild, 3 is spicy—See Glossary and **Tips**)

1½ tablespoons freshly squeezed lime juice

1 teaspoon finely grated lime zest (See **Zesting Citrus Fruits** in Basic Techniques Appendix)

Vegetables
2 carrots, julienned (See Glossary)

1 bunch green onions, bias cut into 1" pieces (both white and green parts)

1 red onion, halved and thinly sliced

2 cups broccoli florets

2 cups snow peas, trimmed

1 red bell pepper, sliced into ¼" wide strips

3 cups assorted mushrooms, cut into ¼" slices

1 bok choy, thinly sliced, or 1 napa cabbage, shredded

WINE PICKS
WHITE ...... *German Riesling*
RED .... *Pinot Noir*

Advance Preparation: *1 hour*

Combine all oil infusion ingredients in a small bowl and stir, making sure oil completely covers ginger and garlic. Cover and refrigerate at least 30 minutes or up to 2 days. Combine all sauce ingredients in a bowl and whisk together until thoroughly blended. Cover and refrigerate at least 30 minutes or up to 2 days. Prepare vegetables as specified. ***Sauce and oil infusion may be prepared <u>up to 2 days in advance</u> if refrigerated. Vegetables may be prepared <u>up to 8 hours in advance</u> if refrigerated.***

Final Preparation: *20 minutes*

1. Heat a large stir-fry pan or large pot over high heat. Add oil infusion and stir-fry until garlic turns golden, about 1 minute. Add all vegetables in the order listed, stirring continuously and allowing about 45–60 seconds between each addition. Add sauce and stir thoroughly.

2. Meanwhile, cook pasta in plenty of rapidly boiling salted water until *al dente*. Drain quickly, and while still dripping, add directly to stir-fry <u>immediately</u> after adding sauce. Reduce heat to medium and toss gently to entangle pasta and vegetables. If mixture is too dry, add some pasta cooking water and toss again. Warm through 2–3 minutes, tossing frequently. Serve immediately straight from the pan with additional soy sauce at the table if desired.

Chris Gluck

NUTRITION DATA
(per serving)

Calories: **450**
Calories from Fat: **19.9%**
Total Fat: **10.3 g**
Saturated Fat: **0.9 g**
Cholesterol: **0 mg**
Sodium: **978 mg**
Carbohydrates: **76 g**
Dietary Fiber: **9.4 g**
Protein: **17 g**

Caramelized Sweet Onion Sauce

Serves 4–6

Don't be alarmed by the seemingly large amount of onions in this recipe. By slowly cooking lots of sweet onions in a small amount of olive oil they soon shrink drastically in size as they sweat in their own juices. Eventually they meld together into a wonderfully sweet and buttery sauce. This alone makes for a delicious pasta topping, or, as I did with this recipe, you can take it a step further with the addition of Italian seasoning, balsamic vinegar and tomatoes.

Pasta

linguine, fettuccine or pasta of your choice
(1 pound dried or 1¼ pounds fresh)

Sauce

2 tablespoons olive oil

2 pounds (about 7 cups) <u>*sweet*</u> *onions, thinly sliced (See* **Tips** *on next page)*

2 tablespoons Italian seasoning

3 tablespoons balsamic vinegar

1 (28 oz.) can diced tomatoes

¼ cup freshly grated Parmesan

Advance Preparation: *10 minutes*

Peel and slice onions. **Ingredients may be prepared <u>up to 8 hours in advance</u> if refrigerated.**

Final Preparation: *2 hours (30 minutes of work)*

1. Heat olive oil in a large pot over high heat. Add onions and cook 10 minutes, stirring frequently.

2. Reduce heat to low and add Italian seasoning. Cook 1 hour, or until onions brown, stirring occasionally. Onions are ready when they begin sticking to the pot, but still scrape up easily. Do not let them burn.

3. Increase heat momentarily and add balsamic vinegar to deglaze (See Glossary) pot. Immediately add tomatoes, juice and all. Bring to a simmer, reduce heat to low and cook 45 minutes, stirring occasionally.

WINE PICKS

WHITE .... *Gewurztraminer*
RED .... *Grenache*

58

4. Meanwhile, cook pasta in plenty of rapidly boiling salted water until *al dente.* Drain and place into a large pre-heated serving bowl. Pour sauce over, toss and serve immediately. Sprinkle Parmesan over each serving at the table.

Chris Gluck

TIPS, HINTS & SHORT-CUTS

Make sure to use <u>sweet</u> onions! The most famous sweet onion is, of course, the Vidalia. Some other common varieties are Texas 1015, Maui, Walla Walla and Inka Sweets. If these are unavailable, ask your grocer or farmers' market vendor for recommendations. Many farmers now grow local varieties that work just as well. Or, in a pinch, you can always mail order Vidalia onions by dialing (800) VIDALIA (843-2542).

NUTRITION DATA
(per serving)

Calories: **474**
Calories from Fat: **16.4%**
Total Fat: **8.7 g**
Saturated Fat: **1.8 g**
Cholesterol: **3 mg**
Sodium: **1014 mg**
Carbohydrates: **83 g**
Dietary Fiber: **6.4 g**
Protein: **16 g**

Twice-Cooked Penne in a Carrot Reduction

Serves 4

Gnocchi (Italian potato dumplings) may be substituted for the pasta. You'll need about 1½ pounds—double the amount of pasta. Gnocchi are available fresh frozen or vacuum packed in shelf-stable packages in most grocery stores. Cook them in boiling salted water as per package directions. Once done, immediately add them to the hot oil in step #3 and stir-fry just like the penne. Then, instead of tossing them with the sauce, first portion out the vegetables from the sauce onto 4 plates. Use a slotted spoon so the carrot liquid stays behind. Next place the stir-fried gnocchi on top of the vegetables. Finally, drizzle over the remaining carrot liquid.

WINE PICKS

WHITE ......German Riesling
RED.....................Pinot Noir

Pasta

penne (¾ pound dried) or gnocchi (1½ pounds—See sidebar notes at left)

Sauce

1½ tablespoons olive oil (divided use)

1 large shallot, minced

1½ tablespoons garlic, minced (divided use)

3 bell peppers (one each of red, green and yellow; or all red), sliced lengthwise into ¼" wide strips

1 medium carrot, julienned (See Glossary)

2 medium zucchini, peeled and cut into strips about the size of a typical French fry

2 cups (about 4 ozs.) shiitake mushroom caps, sliced into ¼" strips (See Glossary)

2 cups fresh home-juiced or store-bought carrot juice (See **Tips** on next page)

1½ tablespoons dill (divided use)

salt and pepper, to taste

Advance Preparation: *30–45 minutes*

Cook pasta in plenty of rapidly boiling salted water until *al dente*. Drain and rinse thoroughly with cold water. Set aside. (Toss pasta with a little olive oil to coat lightly and prevent sticking if cooking well in advance of final preparation.) Prepare vegetables as specified. Juice fresh carrots if preparing juice at home. **Ingredients may be prepared <u>up to 8 hours in advance</u> if refrigerated, although carrot juice tastes best when juiced immediately prior to use.**

Final Preparation: *30 minutes*

1. Heat ½ tablespoon olive oil in a large non-stick skillet or stir-fry pan over medium-high heat. Add shallots and 1 tablespoon garlic. Sauté 1 minute. Immediately add bell peppers and sauté until soft, about 3–4 minutes. Add carrots, zucchini and mushrooms and sauté 3–4 minutes longer. Stir constantly, adding carrot juice at any time if necessary to prevent scorching.

2. Increase heat to high. Deglaze pan with ¼ cup carrot juice. Add ¾ tablespoon dill. As carrot juice reduces, replenish it ¼–½ cup at a time, stirring almost constantly. Continue this process of reducing-replenishing, reducing-replenishing, until all juice is used. At this point there should be about ½–¾ cup of very highly concentrated carrot juice left in the pan. Remove pan from heat but keep warm.

3. Meanwhile, heat remaining 1 tablespoon olive oil in a large stir-fry pan or pot over high heat. Add remaining ½ tablespoon garlic and sauté 30 seconds. Immediately add reserved cooked pasta and remaining ¾ tablespoon dill. Cook on high heat, stirring constantly, until pasta crisps and browns lightly, about 5–7 minutes.

4. After pasta crisps, reduce heat to low and add carrot sauce directly to pasta. Toss and heat through 2–3 minutes. Season to taste with salt and pepper if desired. Serve immediately straight from the pan.

Daniel McKenna

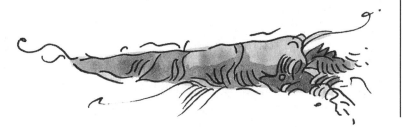

TIPS, HINTS & SHORT-CUTS

If you own a juicer, make your own carrot juice with fresh carrots. You'll need about 2 pounds of carrots to yield 2 cups of juice. Fresh carrot juice is also available in most grocery stores and practically all health food stores. Look for it in the refrigerated section.

NUTRITION DATA
(per serving)

Calories: **561**

Calories from Fat: **11.3%**

Total Fat: **7.3 g**

Saturated Fat: **1.1 g**

Cholesterol: **0 mg**

Sodium: **59 mg**

Carbohydrates: **112 g**

Dietary Fiber: **9.8 g**

Protein: **18 g**

Artichoke & White Wine Sauce

Serves 4–6

Here's a simple and versatile dish typical of Italy's Piedmonte region. It can be served alone as a light and tasty vegetarian entree, or as a refreshing side dish for grilled seafood or chicken.

Pasta

linguine, fettuccine or pasta shape of your choice (1 pound dried or 1¼ pounds fresh)

Sauce

*1 (8 oz.) package frozen artichoke hearts, thawed, or the equivalent amount of fresh artichokes (about 5 medium-sized), trimmed, with the choke removed (See **Tips**)*

juice from 2 lemons (divided use)

2 tablespoons olive oil

2 cloves garlic, left whole

1 yellow onion, thinly sliced

1½ cups dry white wine (divided use)

½ bunch Italian parsley, chopped

salt and pepper, to taste

Advance Preparation: *10 minutes*

Juice lemons. Slice onion. **Ingredients may be prepared up to 8 hours in advance if refrigerated.**

Final Preparation: *45 minutes*

1. Thinly slice artichoke hearts. Place in a bowl and immediately toss with juice from 1½ lemons. Reserve.

2. Heat olive oil in a non-reactive sauté pan or skillet over medium heat. Add garlic, onion and drained artichoke slices. Sauté 3–5 minutes, or until onions begin to turn golden but do not brown. Immediately deglaze pan with ½ cup wine. Allow wine to evaporate, stirring frequently to prevent scorching.

WINE PICKS

WHITE .... *Chardonnay*
RED .... *Beaujolais*

3. The instant wine evaporates, add remaining wine and lemon juice. Season to taste with salt and pepper if desired. Reduce heat to low and simmer, covered, for 20 minutes, or until artichokes are tender. Remove garlic cloves and add parsley.

4. Meanwhile, cook pasta in plenty of rapidly boiling salted water until *al dente*. Drain, reserving ½ cup pasta water. Place pasta in a large, pre-heated serving bowl. Pour sauce over and toss. If pasta appears too dry, add some reserved pasta water and toss again. Serve immediately, grinding black pepper over each serving at the table if desired.

Frank Garofolo

Orzo Vegetable Melange

Serves 4–6

Similar to a vegetarian risotto, only less complicated to make, this versatile one pot dish can be adapted to feature any or all of your favorite vegetables.

Pasta
orzo (1 pound dried)

Vegetables *(See Tips for substitutions and options.)*
½ pound mushrooms of your choice, quartered
6 cloves garlic, minced
1 red onion, quartered, then thinly sliced
1 large carrot, julienned (See Glossary)
¼ pound snow peas, ends trimmed
1 red bell pepper, sliced lengthwise into ¼" wide strips
2 small zucchini, cut into ¼" thick slices
½ pound asparagus, bias cut into 1" pieces
1 ounce sun-dried tomatoes (not oil-packed), chopped

Sauce
2 tablespoons olive oil (divided use)
*5 cups roasted vegetable stock (See **Vegetable Stock Recipes** in Appendix and **Tips**)*
2 tablespoons dried basil, rosemary or herb(s) of your choice
salt and pepper, to taste
¼ cup freshly grated Parmesan

Advance Preparation: *40 minutes*
    Prepare vegetables as specified. ***Ingredients may be prepared <u>up to 24 hours in advance</u> if refrigerated.***

WINE PICKS
WHITE ..... *Sauvignon Blanc*
RED.......................... *Merlot*

Final Preparation: *45 minutes (30 minutes of work)*
    1. Heat 1 tablespoon olive oil in a large pot over high heat until smoking hot. Immediately add mushrooms

and stir constantly until browned, about 5–10 minutes. Remove and reserve mushrooms.

2. Heat remaining 1 tablespoon olive oil in same pot over high heat. Immediately add all remaining vegetables except sun-dried tomatoes and cook 10 minutes, stirring almost constantly.

3. Add reserved mushrooms, sun-dried tomatoes, stock, seasonings and orzo. Reduce heat to medium and stir frequently until stock comes to a simmer. Reduce heat to low and stir constantly until orzo absorbs most of the stock. (See **Cooking Perfect Orzo** in *Basic Techniques Appendix.*) Turn off heat, cover pot and wait 15 minutes.

4. After 15 minutes, stir orzo to make sure all stock is absorbed. Serve immediately, sprinkling Parmesan over each serving at the table.

Chris Gluck

TIPS, HINTS & SHORT-CUTS

Although roasted vegetable stock is preferred for its richer flavor, regular vegetable stock may be used in a pinch. Green onions or leeks may be substituted for the red onion. Many other types of vegetables may also be substituted or added. Try roasted garlic, string beans, squash, cherry tomato halves, corn—just about anything. Or, cut back on the variety and use just a few of your favorite vegetables in larger quantities. One of my favorite versions uses only shiitake mushrooms, asparagus and leeks.

NUTRITION DATA
(per serving)

Calories: **491**
Calories from Fat: **15.6%**
Total Fat: **8.7 g**
Saturated Fat: **1.8 g**
Cholesterol: **3 mg**
Sodium: **234 mg**
Carbohydrates: **86 g**
Dietary Fiber: **7.8 g**
Protein: **19 g**

Mushroom & Red Wine Sauce

Serves 4

This intensely flavored mushroom sauce can also be used as a delicious gravy for grilled foods. Or try adding equal amounts of homemade vegetable stock and cream to make a cream of mushroom soup like you'll never find in a can!

Pasta
fusilli or other spiral shaped pasta of your choice
(½ pound dried)

Sauce
1 cup dry red wine

1 cup vegetable stock (See **Vegetable Stock Recipes** in Appendix)

2 tablespoons oyster sauce (See Glossary)

1 tablespoon soy sauce

2 teaspoons tomato paste (See Glossary)

¼ teaspoon red pepper flakes

½ teaspoon sugar

thyme (1 teaspoon dried or 1 tablespoon fresh)

Vegetables
1 tablespoon canola oil

2 small yellow onions, chopped

4 cloves garlic, minced

1½ pounds mushrooms, cut into ¼" wide strips (See **Tips**)

1 tablespoon cornstarch mixed with 1 tablespoon water

½ cup Italian parsley, chopped

¼ cup freshly grated Parmesan

Advance Preparation: *30 minutes*

Combine all sauce ingredients in a bowl and whisk together until blended. Cover and refrigerate until use. Prepare vegetables as specified. Mix cornstarch and water together. ***Ingredients may be prepared up to 8 hours in advance if refrigerated.***

WINE PICKS
WHITE .... *N/A*
RED.....................*Pinot Noir*

Final Preparation: *1 hour*

1. Heat a large stir-fry pan or large pot over medium heat. Add oil and onions and cook, stirring frequently, until onions turn golden, about 15 minutes. Add a splash of water to prevent scorching if necessary.

2. Add garlic and mushrooms and cook, stirring occasionally, until mushrooms soften and shrink drastically in size, about 20–30 minutes.

3. Add reserved wine sauce and simmer 5 minutes. Stir in cornstarch and simmer 2–3 minutes to thicken.

4. Meanwhile, cook pasta in plenty of rapidly boiling salted water until *al dente*. Drain and add directly to sauce. Toss gently and warm through 2–3 minutes. Season to taste with salt and pepper if desired. Add parsley and toss again. Serve immediately straight from the pan, sprinkling Parmesan over each serving at the table.

Hugh Carpenter

NUTRITION DATA
(per serving)

Calories: *421*

Calories from Fat: *16.1%*

Total Fat: *7.0 g*

Saturated Fat: *1.5 g*

Cholesterol: *5 mg*

Sodium: *804 mg*

Carbohydrates: *66 g*

Dietary Fiber: *5.4 g*

Protein: *17 g*

Roasted Vegetables

ROASTING is an extremely effective cooking method for extracting maximum flavor while using zero or minimal fat. This is especially true when it comes to vegetables, where you can win two ways. First, the dry heat evaporates some of the water present in all vegetables, thereby concentrating the flavors that remain. Second, as the natural sugars also present begin to caramelize in the heat, they add a delicious dimension of rich sweetness to the already concentrated flavors.

All of the recipes that follow can be roasted conventionally in an oven or under a broiler, or, my favorite way, outdoors in a covered barbecue. The barbecue method adds a delicious smoky flavor and is especially nice for those hot summer evenings when you don't feel like heating up the kitchen.

Here's a salsa using broiled tomatoes instead of raw; a grilled vegetable medley that cleans out your refrigerator while making dinner; a versatile red bell pepper pesto that doubles as a dip; a New Mexico pepper sauce utilizing three different types of peppers; a Moroccan-style pasta salad combining roasted peppers and roasted tomatoes; a rich roasted squash sauce pureed with ginger and finished with a splash of sherry; and an Asian-style sauce that solves the age-old problem of oil-saturated eggplant.

Pasta with Roasted Tomato Salsa

Serves 4

Spicy Asian flavors and a deep richness from the concentrated sweetness of roasted tomatoes magically blend together in this especially delicious and unusual salsa. For best results, make sure to use only the highest quality vine-ripened tomatoes.

Pasta

linguine, fettuccine or pasta of your choice (¾ pound dried or 1 pound fresh)

Salsa

3 pounds vine-ripened tomatoes, cut into ½" thick slices

1½ tablespoons sugar (divided use)

½ cup green onions (both white and green parts), chopped

½ cup fresh cilantro, chopped

¼ cup fresh basil, chopped

4 cloves garlic, minced

1 tablespoon ginger root, grated (See Glossary)

3 tablespoons red wine vinegar

1 tablespoon dark sesame oil (See Glossary)

1 teaspoon canola oil

½ –1½ teaspoons (to taste) Chinese chili paste (See Glossary) or red pepper flakes (½ is mild, 1½ is hot)

½ teaspoon salt

Advance Preparation: *1 hour plus time for flavors to blend*
Lightly dust tomato slices with ¾ tablespoon sugar. Place tomatoes on an elevated cake rack in a cookie sheet pan. Broil approximately 4" from heat until golden, about 3 minutes. Turn tomatoes over and repeat on opposite side. (See **Tips** for another method.) Place tomatoes on a plate to cool. Prepare remaining vegetables and herbs as specified. When tomatoes are cool enough to handle, pull off and discard skins. Coarsely chop remaining flesh, taking care to reserve juices. Combine tomatoes, their

WINE PICKS
WHITE .... *Fumé Blanc*
RED.......................*Zinfandel*

70

juices, remaining ¾ tablespoon sugar and all salsa ingredients in a large bowl. Stir, cover and leave at room temperature 30 minutes to allow flavors to marry. **Salsa may be prepared <u>up to 8 hours in advance</u> if refrigerated.**

Final Preparation: *15 minutes*

1. Heat salsa to a simmer in a large, non-reactive pot. Meanwhile, cook pasta in plenty of rapidly boiling salted water until *al dente*. Drain and add pasta directly to salsa. Toss gently and heat through 1–2 minutes. Serve immediately straight from the pot.

Hugh Carpenter

TIPS, HINTS & SHORT-CUTS

The tomatoes can also be grilled on an outdoor barbecue. This will add another delicious smoky flavor dimension to this already complexly flavored sauce. To help prevent the tomatoes from sticking to the grill, spray the grates first with vegetable oil cooking spray.

NUTRITION DATA
(per serving)

*Calories: **463***
*Calories from Fat: **13.6%***
*Total Fat: **7.2 g***
*Saturated Fat: **0.9 g***
*Cholesterol: **0 mg***
*Sodium: **311 mg***
*Carbohydrates: **88 g***
*Dietary Fiber: **6.4 g***
*Protein: **15 g***

Grilled Vegetable Medley with Pasta

Serves 4–6

We first served this dish at our annual 4th of July party years ago. Having just returned from an especially productive (translate "binge") farmers' market spree, and frustrated by our lack of refrigerator space, we decided to make room by getting rid of a rapidly multiplying accumulation of specialty vinegars, oils and other dressings. Ever the Spartans, however, we couldn't bring ourselves to just throw them away—so we mixed everything together to create an impromptu marinade. We brushed the concoction on our bounty of vegetables, threw them on the grill and crossed our fingers. The results were fantastic! We tossed the vegetables with some pasta, added a little fresh garlic—and a new 4th of July tradition was born!

WINE PICKS
WHITE ..... *Sauvignon Blanc*
RED .... *Pinot Noir*

Pasta
*linguine, fettuccine, farfalle or pasta of your choice
(1 pound dried or 1¼ pounds fresh)*

Marinade
*(**Make approximately 1 cup per 4–6 servings**)*
1 part olive oil or ??? (See sidebar)
2 parts balsamic or red wine vinegar or ??? (See sidebar)

Vegetables
*(**Use as many different kinds as possible. Allow 6–7
cups uncooked per 4–6 servings.**)*
whole green onions, cleaned and trimmed
yellow Italian squash, sliced in half lengthwise
whole fresh asparagus, cleaned and trimmed
red onions, cut into thick slices
*large portobello mushroom caps (and/or) whole
mushrooms of your choice*
zucchini, sliced in half lengthwise
carrots, sliced in half lengthwise
Japanese eggplant, sliced in half lengthwise
bell peppers (your choice of colors), sliced into quarters
broccoli spears, cleaned and trimmed
*large ripe tomatoes, halved or quartered (and/or)
cherry tomatoes, left whole*

Sauce
1½ tablespoons olive oil
6 cloves garlic, minced
½ cup fresh basil, chiffonade (See Glossary)
¼ cup freshly grated Parmesan

72

Advance Preparation: *15–30 minutes*

Combine marinade ingredients and whisk together until blended. Prepare vegetables as specified. Chiffonade basil at the last minute. ***Ingredients may be prepared up to 8 hours in advance if refrigerated. Marinade can be made anytime. It will keep for months in the refrigerator.***

Final Preparation: *45 minutes*

1. Spray a clean, cold grill with cooking spray or wipe with a cooking oil-soaked paper towel. This will help prevent the more delicate vegetables from sticking. Turn on heat (or light coals) to pre-heat the grill. Use a broiler if you don't own an outdoor grill.

2. While grill heats, brush vegetables with marinade. Season to taste with salt and pepper if desired.

3. Grill vegetables over medium-hot heat until nicely browned on all sides, turning as necessary. Remove, cut into bite-size pieces and reserve. If using a broiler, place vegetables on an elevated cake rack in a cookie sheet pan and proceed as above.

4. Meanwhile, cook pasta in plenty of rapidly boiling salted water until *al dente*. Drain and place into an extra large serving bowl. Add olive oil and toss. Add garlic and fresh herbs and toss again. Add grilled vegetables and toss a final time. Sprinkle with Parmesan. Serve immediately while still warm, or allow to cool and serve at room temperature. (See ***Cooling Pasta for Salads*** in *Basic Techniques Appendix*.)

Chris Gluck

TIPS, HINTS & SHORT-CUTS

You can also grill extra vegetables to make a delicious vegetarian pizza. Spread a thick layer of tomato sauce (See Basic Marinara Sauce recipe on page 40) over homemade or store-bought pizza crusts, add grilled vegetables, sprinkle with grated Parmesan and/or Mozzarella and bake in a 400° oven until cheese melts and lightly browns.

♦ ♦ ♦ ♦ ♦

Extra grilled vegetables may also be arranged on a platter, drizzled with marinade and served as a warm or cold appetizer.

APPROXIMATE NUTRITION DATA
(per serving)

Calories: **465**
Calories from Fat: **17.7%**
Total Fat: **9.2 g**
Saturated Fat: **1.9 g**
Cholesterol: **3 mg**
Sodium: **89 mg**
Carbohydrates: **80 g**
Dietary Fiber: **5.5 g**
Protein: **16 g**

Roasted Red Bell Pepper Pesto

Yields About 2½ Cups (Enough for 2½ lbs. Pasta)

Make multiple batches of this versatile sauce when red bell peppers are inexpensive and plentiful during the summer months. Divide the excess into 1 cup portions and freeze in zipper lock plastic freezer bags. Then, on the next cloudy winter day, thaw a package or two to bring back some instant summer sunshine!

Pasta
(For 4–6 servings)
pasta of your choice (1 pound dried or 1¼ pounds fresh)

Pesto
(Makes 2½ cups—Use 1 cup per 4–6 servings)
1½ –2 pounds large, "meaty" red bell peppers (to yield 1½ cups roasted peppers)
½ cup freshly grated Parmesan
3/8 cup pecans, roughly chopped
1 heaping tablespoon garlic, roughly chopped
½ cup (tightly packed) cilantro leaves
¼ cup olive oil

Advance Preparation: *60 minutes (15 minutes plus thawing time if using already roasted peppers)*
Roast and peel peppers, reserving juices. (See **Roasting Peppers** in *Basic Techniques Appendix*.) Chop pecans and garlic. Clean cilantro and separate into sprigs. Blend olive oil with ¼ cup of reserved pepper juices. ***Ingredients may be prepared up to 8 hours in advance if refrigerated. Peppers may be roasted and peeled up to 6 months in advance if frozen. (Entire pesto may be prepared completely in advance as per step #1 below and refrigerated up to 4 days or frozen up to 6 months.)***

Final Preparation: *10 minutes*

1. Combine peppers, Parmesan, pecans, garlic and cilantro in a food processor fitted with a steel blade. Pulse (start and stop the blade for a few seconds)

Wine Picks
White .... Chardonnay
Red .... Merlot

74

several times to rough chop and mix ingredients. Drizzle in reserved olive oil/pepper juice mixture at intervals, pulsing each time. Scrape down processor bowl as necessary to combine ingredients. Process until pecans are very finely minced but not liquefied.

2. Meanwhile, cook pasta in plenty of rapidly boiling salted water until *al dente*. Drain and toss with 1 cup of pesto. Season to taste with salt if desired. Serve immediately.

Chris Gluck

NUTRITION DATA
(per serving)

Calories: **431**
Calories from Fat: **19.0%**
Total Fat: **9.1 g**
Saturated Fat: **1.6 g**
Cholesterol: **3 mg**
Sodium: **70 mg**
Carbohydrates: **73 g**
Dietary Fiber: **3.8 g**
Protein: **14 g**

Fire-Roasted New Mexico Pepper Sauce

Serves 4

The wonderful aroma of roasting green chiles permeates the southern New Mexico air during harvest time. Most households in the area roast and freeze large amounts of these chiles to be used throughout the year. Roasting is done at home on outdoor barbecues, on the stove top or in make-shift fires. Some supermarkets even have large roasting drums set up in their parking lots where customers can conveniently roast their just purchased sacks of chiles before taking them home to freeze.

Pasta

> linguine, fettuccine or pasta of your choice
> (¾ pound dried or 1 pound fresh)

Sauce

> 6 mild green chiles such as the typical "Anaheim" variety (See **Tips** on page 79)
>
> 2 green bell peppers
>
> 2 red bell peppers
>
> 2 orange or yellow bell peppers
>
> 2 tablespoons olive oil (divided use)
>
> 6 cloves garlic, minced
>
> 2 peperoncini (typical deli peppers), stemmed, seeded, rinsed and thinly sliced
>
> ¼ cup vegetable stock (See **Vegetable Stock Recipes** in Appendix) or dry white wine
>
> ½ cup Italian parsley, minced
>
> ½ teaspoon ground black pepper
>
> salt, to taste
>
> ¼ cup freshly grated Parmesan

Advance Preparation: *1 hour (15 minutes plus thawing time if using already roasted peppers)*

Roast and peel chiles and bell peppers, reserving juices. (See **Roasting Peppers** in *Basic Techniques Appendix*.) Slice roasted peppers into long thin strips. Prepare remaining ingredients as specified. **Ingredients may be prepared <u>up to 8 hours in advance</u> if refrigerated. Peppers may be roasted and peeled <u>up to 6 months in advance</u> if frozen.**

Wine Picks

White ....Riesling
Red........................... Syrah

Final Preparation: *20 minutes*

1. Heat 1 tablespoon olive oil in a large pan over medium heat. Add garlic and cook until golden, about 2 minutes.

2. Increase heat to high. Immediately add peperoncini and roasted pepper strips along with their juices. Cook 2 minutes, stirring constantly.

3. Add stock (or wine), parsley and black pepper. Reduce heat to medium and cook until liquids almost evaporate. Remove from heat and stir in remaining 1 tablespoon olive oil.

4. Meanwhile, cook pasta in plenty of rapidly boiling salted water until *al dente*. Drain and place into a large serving bowl. Add pepper mixture and toss thoroughly. Season to taste with additional salt if desired. Serve immediately, sprinkling Parmesan over each serving at the table.

Adelina Willem

NUTRITION DATA
(per serving)

*Calories: **495***
*Calories from Fat: **18.8%***
*Total Fat: **10.6 g***
*Saturated Fat: **2.2 g***
*Cholesterol: **4 mg***
*Sodium: **244 mg***
*Carbohydrates: **85 g***
*Dietary Fiber: **6.3 g***
*Protein: **18 g***

Moroccan Roasted Pepper Pasta Sauce

Serves 4–6

Pasta

fusilli, or spiral-shaped pasta of your choice
(1 pound dried or 1¼ pounds fresh)

Sauce

4 bell peppers, your choice of colors (See **Tips**)

4 medium tomatoes

3 green onions (both white and green parts), thinly sliced

Dressing

1½ tablespoons olive oil

2 tablespoons fresh-squeezed orange juice

1 tablespoon fresh-squeezed lemon juice

½ teaspoon ground cumin

¼ teaspoon ground cinnamon

¼ teaspoon ground black pepper

1 jalapeño pepper, seeded and minced (See **Working with Hot Peppers** in *Basic Techniques Appendix*)

2 cloves garlic, minced

1 tablespoon fresh herbs (your choice of cilantro, parsley and/or mint), minced

Advance Preparation: *1 hour*

Roast and peel peppers, reserving juices. (See **Roasting Peppers** in *Basic Techniques Appendix*.) Slice roasted peppers into bite-size strips. Roast and peel tomatoes in the same manner as peppers, reserving juices. Chop into small chunks. Slice green onions as specified. Combine all dressing ingredients and whisk together until blended. *Ingredients may*

WINE PICKS
WHITE .... *Gewurztraminer*
RED .... *Grenache*

be prepared <u>up to 8 hours in advance</u> if refrigerated. Peppers may be roasted and peeled <u>up to 6 months in advance</u> if frozen.

Final Preparation: *1½ hours (15 minutes of work)*

1. Combine peppers, tomatoes and onions in a large bowl. Add dressing and toss thoroughly. Marinate at room temperature at least 1 hour, but no longer than 3 hours. Stir occasionally.

2. Cook pasta in plenty of rapidly boiling salted water until *al dente*. Drain and toss with pepper mixture. Spread out on a baking sheet to cool rapidly. (See **Cooling Pasta for Salads** in *Basic Techniques Appendix*.) When cooled to room temperature, place in a large bowl and serve.

Arlyn Hackett

TIPS, HINTS & SHORT-CUTS

Don't limit yourself to using only bell peppers. Try different types or combinations. Some good candidates are: mild green chiles, Anaheim chiles, Italian peppers and chile poblanos. Keep in mind, however, that there are hundreds of different peppers—some with very limited regional availability. If these particular varieties aren't available, experiment with those indigenous to your part of the country.

NUTRITION DATA
(per serving)

*Calories: **449***
*Calories from Fat: **12.2%***
*Total Fat: **6.2 g***
*Saturated Fat: **0.9 g***
*Cholesterol: **0 mg***
*Sodium: **33 mg***
*Carbohydrates: **85 g***
*Dietary Fiber: **7.0 g***
*Protein: **15 g***

Roasted Squash Sauce with Ginger & Sherry

Serves 4–6

This sauce also doubles as a delicious vegetable bisque. Make extra sauce without adding the sherry. Then serve in soup bowls just as it is, or slightly diluted with vegetable stock and/or cream. Add a splash of sherry at the table and sprinkle a little cilantro over the top. Or, for a more festive presentation, cut only the tops off the squash, instead of cutting them into strips. Scoop out the seeds and bake the whole squash. Then carefully scrape out the baked squash, leaving ¼" or so intact with the outer skin. Use the baked squash in the recipe and the hollowed-out shells as individual serving bowls.

Pasta

pasta of your choice (1 pound dried or 1¼ pounds fresh)

Sauce

2 pounds winter squash (to yield 2 cups cooked), seeded and cut into 1" wide strips (See **Tips**)

3 tablespoons olive oil (divided use)

1 whole garlic bulb

2 cups yellow or sweet onions, chopped

3 tablespoons ginger root, minced (See Glossary)

3 cups roasted or regular vegetable stock (See **Vegetable Stock Recipes** in Appendix)

½ cup (or more, to taste) cream sherry

½ cup cilantro, minced

2 limes, quartered

Advance Preparation: *1–1¼ hours*

Clean and cut squash into strips as specified. Brush flesh with 2 teaspoons olive oil. Place squash in a heavy roasting pan, making sure individual strips don't touch each other. Roast at 375° until soft, about 25–40 minutes. Roast garlic along with squash. (See ***Roasting Garlic*** in *Basic Techniques Appendix*.) Alternatively, roast squash and garlic (in a roasting pan) in a covered outdoor barbecue over medium heat. When cool enough to handle, peel squash and cut into cubes. Squeeze roasted garlic cloves out of their skins and reserve. While squash and garlic roast, cook onion in 1 teaspoon olive oil in a covered saucepan over low heat 20 minutes, stirring

WINE PICKS

WHITE .... *Chardonnay*
RED.................... *Pinot Noir*

occasionally. Add a splash of water if necessary to prevent scorching. Remove cover and continue cooking on low until onions turn golden, about 15–20 minutes. Stir as necessary to prevent burning. When onions turn golden, add ginger and cook 5 minutes longer, stirring frequently. Remove from heat and reserve. Puree 2 cups roasted squash cubes, roasted garlic, onion mixture, vegetable stock and remaining 2 tablespoons olive oil in a blender on high speed until silky smooth, about 2 minutes. This will need to be done in stages depending on the size of your blender. **Ingredients may be prepared <u>up to 2 days in advance</u> if refrigerated. See additional notes at step #1 below.**

Final Preparation: *20 minutes*

1. Cook squash puree in a large saucepan over very low heat 15 minutes, stirring frequently. (The complex, caramelized, slow-roasted flavors in this sauce will <u>definitely</u> benefit with additional "flavor blending" time. Time permitting, cook the sauce, let it cool to room temperature, and refrigerate overnight before re-heating the following day.)

2. Add sherry and cook only until sauce is hot again, no more than 3–4 minutes. Salt to taste if desired.

3. Meanwhile, cook pasta in plenty of rapidly boiling salted water until *al dente*. Drain and place into a large serving bowl. Pour sauce over, toss, sprinkle on cilantro and serve immediately. Garnish with lime quarters to squeeze over each serving at the table.

Chris Gluck

NUTRITION DATA
(per serving)

Calories: **543**
Calories from Fat: **16.8%**
Total Fat: **9.8 g**
Saturated Fat: **1.4 g**
Cholesterol: **0 mg**
Sodium: **303 mg**
Carbohydrates: **95 g**
Dietary Fiber: **3.2 g**
Protein: **15 g**

Asian-Style Roasted Eggplant Sauce

Serves 4

Eggplant, notorious for soaking up oil when cooked conventionally, is here baked instead. Baking allows the skin to seal in the heat and steams the eggplant to doneness from the inside out. The now soft but non-oil saturated flesh then readily absorbs this highly flavorful, but lower fat Asian sauce.

Pasta

linguine (¾ pound dried or 1 pound fresh)

1 tablespoon dark sesame oil (See Glossary)

Sauce

1 pound Japanese eggplants

2 tablespoons soy sauce

1 tablespoon balsamic vinegar

1 teaspoon sugar

½ teaspoon dark sesame oil (See Glossary)

1 tablespoon canola oil

3 cloves garlic, minced

½ teaspoon ginger root, minced (See Glossary)

1 jalapeño pepper, stemmed, seeded and finely chopped (See **Working with Hot Peppers** in Basic Techniques Appendix)

1 tomato, seeded and diced

1 tablespoon fresh cilantro, minced

Advance Preparation: *40 minutes*

Pierce eggplants in several places. Bake at 400° until soft, about 30 minutes. Alternatively, grill in a covered outdoor barbecue over low heat, turning occasionally to prevent burning. Slice in half lengthwise and scrape out flesh with a spoon. Chop coarsely and reserve, discarding skins. Combine soy sauce, balsamic vinegar, sugar and ½ teaspoon sesame oil. Mix and reserve. Prepare garlic, ginger, jalapeño and tomato as specified. Mince cilantro at the last minute. ***Ingredients may be prepared <u>up to 8 hours in advance</u> if refrigerated.***

WINE PICKS
(Champagne)
WHITE .... *Extra-Dry*
RED .... *Blanc de Noirs*

Final Preparation: *15 minutes*

1. Heat canola oil in a skillet over medium-high heat. Add garlic, ginger and jalapeño and sauté 1 minute. Remove from heat and stir in soy sauce mixture. Stir in reserved eggplant, tomato and cilantro.

2. Meanwhile, cook pasta in plenty of rapidly boiling salted water until *al dente*. Drain, place into a large serving bowl and toss with 1 tablespoon sesame oil. Add eggplant mixture, toss again and serve. Season to taste with additional soy sauce if desired.

Stella Fong

TIPS, HINTS & SHORT-CUTS

This sauce, without the pasta and final tablespoon of sesame oil, may also be used as a dip for chips or as a tasty condiment for grilled seafood.

NUTRITION DATA
(per serving)

Calories: **435**
Calories from Fat: **18.7%**
Total Fat: **9.1 g**
Saturated Fat: **1.1 g**
Cholesterol: **0 mg**
Sodium: **429 mg**
Carbohydrates: **76 g**
Dietary Fiber: **5.6 g**
Protein: **13 g**

Appendix

Vegetable Stock Recipes

Yields 8 Cups

Stock
3 yellow onions, coarsely chopped
10 celery stalks, coarsely chopped
5 carrots, peeled and coarsely chopped
3 leeks, cleaned and cut into ¼" slices
10 cloves garlic, smashed
2 red bell peppers, seeded and sliced
2 ounces sun-dried tomatoes (optional)
1 pound mushrooms (optional)

Preparation: *2½ hours*

Put all ingredients into a large pot. Add 5 quarts water. Bring to a boil, reduce heat and simmer uncovered 1½ hours. Strain through a colander, pressing down on the vegetables to extract all their juices and flavors. Return stock to pot and simmer until reduced to 2 quarts. Strain through a cheesecloth-lined sieve to clarify. Use or freeze immediately.

Roasted Variation: *3½ hours plus chilling time*

Put ingredients into a pot. Add ½ cup unsalted butter. Cook over medium heat until vegetables wilt and begin to brown, stirring occasionally. At this point stir frequently, scraping up any caramelized vegetable bits. When vegetables are well browned, deglaze with 1 cup water or dry white wine. Add 5 quarts water and proceed as above. After removing vegetables and reducing stock as above, refrigerate until butter solidifies. Discard butter and clarify as above.

Making homemade stock doesn't require much attention, but it does take time. Accordingly, the best time to make stock is when you're going to be in the kitchen doing something else anyway. Because it takes the same amount of effort to make a little or a lot, it's a good idea to make a lot and freeze the excess. This recipe has a relatively large yield for this reason. Divide the excess into 1 cup portions and freeze in zipper lock freezer bags (or empty yogurt or cottage cheese containers). Then, next time a recipe calls for stock, you'll have delicious homemade stock conveniently pre-measured and ready for immediate use.

Miscellaneous Kitchen Notes

Herbs Unless specified fresh, herbs used in this book refer to the dry variety typically sold in small spice jars. EXCEPTION: Always use fresh cilantro, Italian parsley and mint for the recipes in this book. As a general rule, if fresh herbs are available, triple the amount used if substituting for the dry variety.

Kitchen Equipment Following is a list of handy kitchen equipment that will improve and simplify pasta preparation and serving.

- **Pasta Pot** Use a large (8 quart <u>minimum</u> capacity) pasta pot that comes with a colander-like removable insert specially designed for cooking pasta. (See illustration on page 7.) Pasta is cooked inside the insert, which is then lifted out in its entirety from the boiling water when done. This efficient design eliminates the potentially dangerous step of lifting a heavy pot filled with boiling water and draining it into another colander in the sink.

- **Stir-Fry Pan** A large (preferably 14" wide) flat-bottomed stir-fry pan makes it easy to rapidly and efficiently cook large quantities of ingredients. Its larger cooking surface also helps vegetables retain their texture without getting mushy and easily accommodates large amounts of cooked pasta when "saucing in the pan," or adding pasta directly to the sauce.

- **Non-Reactive Sauce Pans** Always use stainless steel or other high-tech alloy or non-stick sauce pans when cooking sauces containing tomatoes or acidic ingredients like citrus or wine. Aluminum or cast iron pans will discolor and can impart an off taste to your sauce.

- **Serving Bowl** Use a shallow, extra-wide serving bowl to serve pasta. The shallowness helps dissipate the internal heat that tends to cause hot pasta to stick together into a gooey mass, while the extra width makes it easier to toss the pasta with its sauce. Always use a ceramic bowl when serving hot pasta dishes as it retains heat better than most other materials. Pre-heat the bowl by filling it with very hot water a few minutes before adding the pasta.

Olive Oil Grades There is much confusion about whether or not one should use extra-virgin olive oil in cooking. It is not specified for any of the recipes in this book because most extra-virgin oils have a distinctive olive taste that can interfere with the rest of the sauce. While some chefs will consider this advice heresy, my recommendation is that you shop around until finding a reasonably priced, neutral tasting olive oil. I think you'll find it quite adequate for cooking. Save the higher priced extra-virgin olive oils for dipping bread, for salad dressings or raw sauces, or for recipes where a distinctive olive flavor is desired.

Dry vs. Fresh Pasta Whenever applicable, quantities for both options are listed. Because fresh pasta has a higher water content, and therefore weighs more for the same volume quantity of dry pasta, it usually requires about 25% more by weight than regular dry pasta. Fresh pasta may be made by hand at home, or purchased in the refrigerated section of most supermarkets. Fresh pastas cook 300–500% faster than dry pastas and are usually available in a myriad of exotic flavors. See Tomato & Garlic Raw Sauce on page 38 for a recipe idea.

Entertaining Tips When cooking pasta for company, do all of the advance preparation steps before your guests arrive. In many cases, the sauce and sometimes even the entire dish can be made in advance. Pasta may also be pre-cooked for ease of last minute preparation. Undercook it slightly and then immediately rinse in cold water. Drain thoroughly, toss lightly with olive or canola oil to prevent sticking and refrigerate in plastic bags. When ready to use, simply cook the pasta in boiling water for a few minutes to heat through.

Stocking Your Pantry Take a few minutes to peruse the recipes that catch your eye. Make a list of the shelf-stable ingredients you don't have. Then go to the store and buy all of them. A good basic list should include: *a large selection of pasta shapes, canola oil, olive oil, sesame oil, rice vinegar, balsamic vinegar, red wine vinegar, canned tomatoes, tomato paste (can and tube variety), soy sauce (regular or low-sodium), capers, red pepper flakes and/or Chinese chili paste, Kalamata and/or oil-cured black olives, oyster sauce (or vegetarian stir-fry sauce), sun-dried tomatoes, honey, cornstarch, bottled hot sauce and brown sugar.* By stocking your pantry with these ingredients now, it'll be easier to make more recipes later and will help in those spur-of-the-moment situations when you need something "right now."

Cooking with Wine While we've all been taught never to cook with wine we wouldn't drink, at $7–8 for an average bottle, 1 cup of wine costs about $2.50. A more affordable solution for cooking is to use box wine. Box wine is sold in air-tight pouches packed inside a box and installed with a dispensing tap. As wine is used, the pouch shrinks around the remaining wine, preventing rapid oxidation and thereby prolonging shelf life. Box wine comes in 3 or 5 liter pouches and is available in most varietals. I use *Chablis* and *Chianti* for recipes calling for dry white and dry red wines respectively. Although these wines will never win any awards from serious connoisseurs, they are certainly adequate for cooking, and at an average cost of about 40¢ per cup, are very affordable.

Nutrition Data Nutrition data is not included for any ingredient marked *optional* or *to taste*, or for the salt and/or oil that may be added to the water used to cook the pasta. Whenever a range of servings is indicated, nutrition data is calculated on the average. For example, if servings are listed as 4–6, nutrition data is computed on 5 servings.

Basic Techniques

Cooling Pasta for Salads Many cold or room temperature pasta salads taste best if prepared with hot (as opposed to rinsed and cooled) pasta. However, if left to cool in a serving bowl, hot pasta will clump together into an unappetizing mess. Remedy this by spreading the hot pasta (after it's been tossed with its sauce or other ingredients) out in a thin layer on a baking sheet or several dinner plates. This allows the heat to dissipate rapidly and lets the pasta cool without clumping. Once cooled, put it back into a serving bowl or container.

Eliminating Bitterness in Eggplant Most eggplants have a slight bitterness that can adversely affect a recipe's outcome. This bitterness is easily eliminated as follows: Peel the eggplant and slice it horizontally into ½" to ¾" thick slices. Sprinkle the slices liberally with salt. Layer the slices in a colander in a sink. Place a clean, heavy object on top to weigh them down. (I use a large pot filled with water.) Leave it on for 30 minutes. After 30 minutes, blot the slices dry with a paper towel and proceed with the recipe.

Roasting Garlic Roasting softens garlic to a jam-like consistency and mellows it to a point of being almost sweet. To roast garlic, take an entire unpeeled head and cut off the top quarter. (Cutting off the tips prevents the cloves from splitting during the roasting process by providing a predetermined release point for the expanding garlic to seep out.) Wrap the garlic in aluminum foil and place cut side up on a pie tin. Bake at 400° for 35–45 minutes, or until the garlic becomes very soft and begins to ooze from the tips. When cool enough to handle, squeeze the now paste-like garlic out of its skin by pinching each clove until the roasted garlic squirts out from the cut end.

Marinating Short-Cut Marinades are flavored liquids used to infuse flavor into meats and vegetables. The items to be marinated are typically placed into a bowl of marinade and then periodically turned to ensure even marinating. A more efficient way is as follows: Place the items and marinade in a plastic zipper lock freezer bag. Seal the bag, leaving a large air pocket inside. Shake it several times to evenly coat the items. Open the bag slightly, "burp" out the air pocket, and seal again, compressing the bag tightly this time. Because the compressed plastic keeps the marinade in contact with all of the items all of the time, they never have to be turned, and you can usually use lots less marinade.

Cooking Perfect Orzo Orzo is a tiny rice-shaped pasta. The most common way to cook it is simply in boiling water like regular pasta. Another, and I think better way, is to cook it in a flavored liquid (like juice, stock or even milk) until it absorbs the liquid. This infuses flavor directly into the pasta and eliminates draining, thereby saving a step. Following are instructions for this method: Use 1½ cups orzo with 2½–3 cups of liquid for 6–10 side dish servings, or 1 pound of orzo with 4–5 cups of liquid for 6–8 main course servings. Exact liquid quantities are not critical as the orzo can be cooked as long as it takes to absorb the liquid. First, heat the liquid in a saucepan or pot over medium heat until warm. Next, reduce the heat to low and add the uncooked orzo. Stir almost constantly until the orzo absorbs almost all of the liquid. (Additional ingredients may be added before or after the orzo. See the recipes on pages 28 and 64 for specific examples.) Next, turn off the heat and cover the pan with a tight fitting lid. Wait 10 minutes, then remove the lid and stir the orzo. All of the liquid should be absorbed by now. If it isn't, cook a few minutes longer on very low heat until it's not runny anymore, stirring constantly to prevent scorching.

Working with Hot Peppers Wear rubber gloves when cleaning and chopping peppers if you have sensitive skin. The inside flesh, seeds and veins of peppers contain oils that can rub into your skin and cause a burning sensation for hours. These same oils can also quickly transfer from your hands to whatever they touch—so make sure not to rub your eyes or touch other sensitive flesh.

Roasting Peppers First, char the peppers until their skins blacken and blister. This can be done on a barbecue, under a broiler, on a grate over an electric burner, or even with tongs over an open flame. Next, sweat the charred peppers in their own heat to loosen their skins by placing them in a large bowl tightly sealed with plastic wrap. When cool enough to handle (about 20 minutes), hold the peppers over the bowl and peel off the skins. This enables you to catch and retain the flavorful pepper juices which will drip out as you're peeling. Resist the temptation to rinse off remaining bits of skin under the faucet as this will wash away much of the flavor. Finally, cut the peeled pepper in half, remove the webs and seeds, and slice as per recipe specifications. Most stores also sell already roasted red bell peppers packed in jars or cans. While these can certainly be used in a pinch, they won't taste quite as good as home roasted.

Peeling Tomatoes Peel tomatoes quickly by first scoring a small "X" opposite the core end and then plunging them into boiling water for 10 seconds. Remove immediately and place into a bowl of ice water. When the tomatoes are cool enough to handle (about 30 seconds), the skins will peel off in seconds.

Zesting Citrus Fruits When grating citrus zest, be extra careful to grate only the top thin colored layer. The white part directly underneath is very bitter and will ruin the flavor of any dish. Most kitchenware stores sell inexpensive citrus zesters designed to cut only through this thin layer. If one is not available, simply use the fine holes on a cheese grater instead.

Glossary

Al dente Italian for "to the tooth," or to cook pasta until it's tender but still firm.

Angel hair (also Spaghettini) Very thin, round pasta strands.

Blanch To briefly plunge food into boiling water and then to immediately rinse in cold water. In addition to slightly pre-cooking food, blanching also helps preserve color and flavor, especially in green vegetables and herbs.

Capers The unopened floral bud of a wild Mediterranean shrub. Usually sold packed in a salty vinegar brine. Use sparingly—a few go a long way.

Chiffonade To slice leafy herbs or vegetables into very fine strips. Best done by first stacking the leaves on top of each other, then rolling them into a tight "cigar," and finally slicing into 1/16" wide strips with a very sharp knife.

Chinese chili paste An extremely hot blend of pureed fresh and dried chiles mixed with vinegar and sometimes other ingredients. Available in Asian markets and some supermarkets. Substitution: Crushed red pepper flakes.

Conchiglie Small pasta shells.

Deglaze The process of releasing the bits of food that caramelize or stick to the bottom of a pan during roasting or sautéing. By adding a liquid (typically stock, juice, wine, spirits or water) to the hot pan, these pan deposits dissolve and release their highly concentrated flavors back into the liquid or sauce.

Farfalle Small, bow tie or butterfly-shaped pasta.

Feta cheese A crumbly, flavorful, lower-calorie Greek cheese. Available in supermarkets.

Fettuccine Flat, ¼" wide pasta strands.

Fusilli Short, corkscrew or spiral-shaped pasta.

Ginger root Not really a root, but an underground stem, or rhizome. It has a unique flavor that can be simultaneously spicy hot and refreshingly cool. First peel the skin with a sharp paring knife; then grate, mince or thinly slice against the grain. Don't substitute powdered ginger. Available in supermarkets.

Gnocchi Tiny Italian potato dumplings about the size of a large garlic clove. Available in most supermarkets in shelf-stable, vacuum-packed packages, or individually quick frozen in the freezer section. Cook in boiling water just until they float; then retrieve with a slotted spoon. See page 60 for more information.

Julienne To cut food into pieces about the size of match sticks.

Kalamata (Greek) olives Ripe olives cured in a salt brine to which vinegar is added upon packing. Readily available canned in supermarkets or bulk in ethnic (Greek, Italian or Middle Eastern) markets and delis.

Linguine Flat, thin pasta strands.

Oil-cured black olives Strong-flavored black olives covered with a thin film of olive oil. Sold loose, not packed in brine. Available in jars in most supermarkets or bulk in ethnic (Greek, Italian or Middle Eastern) markets and delis.

Orzo Tiny, rice-shaped pasta. See *Basic Techniques*.

Oyster sauce A thick, smoky yet sweet Asian sauce. Available in supermarkets. Vegetarian substitution: *Lee Kum Kee* brand *Vegetarian Stir-Fry Sauce*.

Penne Short, 3/8" diameter, tube-shaped pasta.

Radiatore Small, ¾" diameter pasta with protruding wavy, radiator-like fins.

Reduce The process of heating a liquid until a portion of it evaporates, leaving behind a richer, more concentrated liquid.

Rice vinegar A mild, almost sweet, low-acid Asian vinegar. Use sparingly in sauces and marinades. Available in most supermarkets.

Sesame oil A dark, nutty-tasting oil pressed from toasted sesame seeds. Used only for flavoring—not for cooking. Available in most supermarkets.

Shiitake mushrooms A rich, meaty-flavored mushroom. Stem is inedible. Available fresh in most supermarkets or dehydrated in Asian markets.

Spaghetti Thin, round pasta strands.

Sun-dried tomatoes Thin tomato slices dehydrated in the sun or in ovens. Available packed in oil or dry. The oil-packed variety is ready for immediate recipe use. The dry variety must be re-hydrated in hot water for a few minutes.

Sweat To slowly cook food over low heat in a small amount of low-fat or fat-free liquid (typically water, stock, wine or juice). Sometimes a small amount of olive oil or other fat is added to hasten the cooking process and prevent scorching.

Tomato paste Concentrated tomatoes. Traditionally sold in 6 ounce cans. Use the double-concentrated variety packed in a toothpaste-like tube when a recipe calls for a small amount. Leftovers in the tube keep indefinitely if refrigerated.

Zest The thin outer layer of citrus fruit. See *Basic Techniques*.

Index

Order Form

Pasta Press® PO Box 3070, San Diego, CA 92163

- ☐ Please send me the products ordered below.
- ☐ Please put my name on your mailing list for future books.

_____
NAME (PLEASE PRINT)

_____
ADDRESS

_____
CITY   STATE   ZIP

See reverse side for complete product descriptions.

QTY	DESCRIPTION	UNIT PRICE	TOTAL PRICE
	Pasta & Garlic Cookbook	$6.95	
	Pasta & Vegetables Cookbook	$7.95	
	1-Year Pasta Press Subscription (4 Issues)	$9.95	
	Sales Tax (California Only) on Books Only		
	Shipping & Handling (See Chart Below)		
☐ Check Enclosed ☐ Bill My Credit Card Below		**TOTAL**	

☐ **Visa** (13 or 16 digits)   ☐ **MC** (16 digits)   ☐ **Discover** (16 digits)   ☐ **Amer Exp** (15 digits)

| | | | | | | | | | | | | | | | |
1   2   3   4   5   6   7   8   9   10   11   12   13   14   15   16
CREDIT CARD ACCOUNT NUMBER

| | | - | | |
MONTH   (EXPIRATION)   YEAR   AUTHORIZED SIGNATURE

Shipping & Handling (USA Only)

1 Book $2.00
2 or More Books (No Limit!)............. $2.95

Toll Free Order Line (800) 770-2201

*If you enjoyed the recipes in this book, we invite you to subscribe to **Pasta Press**—the magazine that made it all possible!*

Call (800) 770-2201 to order by telephone,
or use the form on the reverse side.

Now, even <u>more</u> low-fat pasta recipes…that work!

Available at your local bookstore or direct from Pasta Press